the
Jew and
His Family

the
Jew and
His Family

Benjamin KAPLAN

Louisiana State University Press
BATON ROUGE

THIS
BOOK IS
DEDICATED
TO "LITTLE JOE," MY AMAZING FATHER, WHO,
WHEN HE LEFT THE DARKNESS OF RECHICHA,
MINSKER GUBERNIA, WENT ON HIS FIRST
JOURNEY WITH THE SAME COURAGE,
DIGNITY, HUMOR, AND FAITH AS
HE DID HIS LAST, AND WHO MUST
BE NOTING WITH DEEP SATISFACTION
THAT HIS CHILDREN ARE DOING THEIR BEST
TO FOLLOW HIS ADMONITION THROUGH THE YEARS:
GO IN PEACE
AND IN
GOD

Preface

While still a child living in the frightful, ghetto-like atmosphere of Eastern Europe, I learned the value and meaning of the family. There by the lamp on weekdays and by candlelight on the Sabbath I learned quickly that people are born for each other, that when one member of the family falls, or sickens, or is trampled by a drunken Russian peasant, there is no need to ask for whom the bell tolls—it tolls for the entire family, yes, even for all mankind.

In that family, truth about life was not told in halves because fear does not come in halves, nor does the whip cut in halves, nor the fire burn in halves, nor death take in halves; and therefore love, confidence, and faith must not come in halves. It was there that I first learned to appreciate the family and the home it created and its influences both for good and for evil. There I discovered the deep value of the love of parents and brothers, the profound feeling of belonging. There was the only place to find security, the only spot which was a cushioned retreat from the weariness of life outside.

There was strength and inspiration in that one-room hut; there was humor, pathos, and a quality of the soul. The Jewish family of that place and time tried to answer the basic question: what is the good in life? It probed into happiness and sadness and the conditions which surround them, into virtue and justice, into one's relation to his neighbor and his God.

Thus our family helped each of us directly and immediately to live better, to bear with greater dignity and fortitude the burdens of human beings living in poverty, fear, cold, and hunger. Family living in those days was indeed precarious, uncertain, and difficult, yet always bound by a genuine and meaningful sense of togetherness, by affection, and by God's eternal blessing.

Many times in the years since that time, a half century ago, all the assurances of that family life have returned to me, all that singular confidence and faith which love within a family can generate and nurture if only it is actuated by freedom and balance, humor and understanding, faith and dedication. There was something unassailable and immovable in such a family—qualities fast disappearing from contemporary life. As a result, a large part of the original rich content of the home has been lost. Instead of remaining a place of much activity, where many things of consequence to the family happen, the home has been transformed into a place in which there is only a limited amount of activity and one which is not overly important.

I have since come to the realization through observation, study, and counseling that behind closed doors and drawn shades the needs, hopes, and dreams of family members may either be successfully fulfilled or they may collide and explode. I have discovered also that there is about family interplay a warm and affectionate rhythm as well as a naked and brutal incisiveness. It is a startling fact that home is where one is either at his best or at his worst.

Of all the institutions which condition behavior and adjustment of the individual, none is more important than the family. Also, of all institutions it is the first in the development of man as a social being. The tragedy is that, despite the truth of the above statement, the family has become a mere cliché today, and our society has taken it for granted, ignored it, shunted it aside, yet expects it to do the nation's molding, patching, and mending without much attention or reward.

I have been intimately involved in the Jewish family for a half century as a participant, as a student of sociology and as a marriage counselor, and I feel a deep sense of urgency about the place of the Jewish family in America today. I also recognize full well the risks and dangers in writing on an illusive subject so close to my heart. Indeed, I have long had the desire to lay my hands on the stuff out of which is made the Jewish family, those cultural elements—including truth, fantasy, tradition, laws, and prophetic beliefs—which have become solidified through the centuries and evolved as a style of living.

The story of the Jewish family I consider a romance, one of the strangest and most colorful sagas of all mankind. Very few people have searched for the meaning of life with such a single mind as have the Jews. I firmly believe that in this drama there is summarized and enobled a group of unusual people.

Despite my sense of urgency about writing this story and my deep conviction about the permanent worth of the Jewish family, I realize that to explore the wonder, the excitement, and triumphant adventure of the Jewish family through the centuries, across the continents and over the seas from Ur, in Chaldea, to Lafayette, in Louisiana, is an undertaking of great magnitude. As an academician there has always been a point beyond which I could not go, but now I undertake this journey. I have put myself into this story frankly and without reservation and have become completely immersed in it. This is no mere documentation; even the tiniest item has been processed by the awareness of the author. There are times when the distinction between what is subjective and objective vanishes. This is not to imply that I do not fully recognize and appreciate the detached and scientific point of view. As a matter of fact I long ago became intrigued with the very essence of the scientific spirit. I was reading in Exodus (3:2–4). The Lord was speaking to Moses personally at the scene of the bush: "And Moses said 'I will turn aside and see *why* the bush is not burnt.'" I have been asking *why* ever since.

Finally, it is the plan of the writer that this story will be neither an emotional portrayal of the Jew and his family colored merely by sympathy nor a self-critical exposure bordering on self-hatred as many stories about the Jews often seem to be. It is, in a sense, a deeply moving account of a sociological theme with an autobiographical base, and only one who has been an intimate part of this theme can write with a sense of urgency and immediacy the epic of a people's struggle to find sense in an often senseless world.

To attempt to analyze and portray the Jewish family from biblical days to the present takes courage or foolhardiness, or perhaps a bit of both. This is understandable when one realizes that it is difficult even to find an acceptable definition of Judaism. At this moment there is raging in Israel a truly serious storm over the definition of a Jew. No wonder, then, that very few sociologists have attempted to deal with the Jewish family.

The Jewish family is complex by virtue of the varied cultural factors which have gone into the making of it, the theological and ethical commitments which infuse it, the special conditions of its many different areas of existence, the objectives and ends which guide it, and the multiplicity of forces impinging upon it from all directions. The essence of this particular theme is that, especially in the case of the Jews, the family process is a flow of family experience from generation to generation, crossing national boundaries, strange languages, and varied cultures, in the course of which its members developed unique ideals, values, expectations, and aspirations.

Where, then, does such a story begin? This is more than an academic question since a story is part of life; and life, whether that of an individual or a people, has neither a beginning nor an ending. Every child who is born into a Jewish home today goes back a thousand generations. He really belongs to no time, no place; he is part of eternal humanity. Yet inevitably he perpetuates the pact which Avrom (Abraham) made with God, and he anticipates the future of all Judaism. However, since man is destined to measure eternity with an alarm clock and to compute infinity with a yardstick, he has to start at a given place and a given time and has to stop at a given place and a given time. As I have noted, this story does just that—

it starts with Avrom in Ur of Chaldea and stops with the writer in Lafayette, Louisiana. I do not imply that this is the whole story of the Jews and their family life, for that is beyond one man's power to tell. No mortal man will ever know the full truth about all that has happened to these incredible people.

The basic conception of the family within which framework it will be studied in this book is that of a unit of interacting and intercommunicating persons enacting the social roles of husband and wife, mother and father, son and daughter, brother and sister—the definition given by Burgess and Locke in their study of the family. As they point out: "The roles are defined by the community but in each family they are powerfully reinforced by sentiments, partly traditional and partly emotional, arising out of experience."[1] This is what may be termed the social psychological approach. An adequate discussion of the nature and development of the Jewish family in the various areas of the Diaspora (dispersal) and in different periods would be beyond the scope of this writer. Therefore the undertaking will be confined to the construction of a "model" (in a sense an empirical abstraction as far as possible), a methodological technique known in sociology as the "ideal" type. The writer hopes thus to take out a slice of Jewish life in three widely separated lands in three greatly separated times and paint pictures of them in broad, deeply colored strokes. Quite naturally, like any picture painted with broad strokes, this one conceals as much as it reveals. The three ideal families chosen are the biblical family, the family of the *shtetl* in nineteenth-century Eastern Europe, and the modern American family.

The biblical family was selected because the biblical climate had more to do with shaping the Hebraic culture and its family structure than did any other time or region. It is a fact that the truth about Jews of biblical days is an illusive thing, but it is also a fact that no one, however highly trained, can argue them out of their personal experiences. The great figures of the Bible—Avrom, Isaac, Jacob,

[1] Ernest W. Burgess and Harvey Locke, *The Family* (New York: American Book Co., 1953), 7.

Moses, David, Solomon, Isaiah, Micah, and Job—have about them
a kind of concreteness and directness, a kind of historicity that can
hardly be questioned. Most of the basic values of the Jewish way of
life have their origins in the Bible. Anthropologists and historians
may disagree on what the Jews were really like then, but the fact remains that the guideposts set up by those people thousands of years
ago continue to this very day to influence the lives of most Jews
throughout the world, as well as the lives of hundreds of millions of
non-Jews.

Actually, in the shtetl (the shtetl was the small, pre-World War I
Jewish community in eastern Europe, semi-isolated from the Christian community around it.) the family was more the focal point of
Jewish life than the synagogue. The Jews of the shtetl were guided
by reflexes which were etched into their makeup too deeply to be
removed. The years of preparation for the business of being Jewish,
the endless hours of learning Torah and of practicing the mental
gymnastics of belonging to a group of eternal strangers solidified the
family and made it the center of their everyday living. The difficulties of the outside world increased the importance of the family as
a repository of human warmth and psychic fulfillment. In order to
maintain their stability, their mental as well as their physical health,
even their very survival, it was necessary to develop a close-knit
family group, well ordered, and religiously oriented.

Most of the shtetl Jews were without worldly experience of any
kind; their total intellectual association was the Torah and the Talmud.
In these books were their history and their philosophy, their poetry
and their songs, their understanding of people and of God, their goals
and their salvation. Members of the shtetl family were certain that
there was intention and purpose in the universe simply because they
felt there was intention and purpose in each one of them, in their
families, and in their God.

In the last few decades the Jewish family in America has been in
transition from an institutional to a companionship form. This transition is, in part, the result of major social changes which have taken
place in the American way of life and which have thus placed this

particular family in a radically different environment from that of the past. Thus it is that many Jews have developed a strange uneasiness and deep anxiety as they discover themselves trapped in a frightening predicament. Oftentimes their very souls long to return to a warmer and more satisfying relationship with their ancient tradition, with the old-time family solidarity, and with the God of their fathers. So very many of them are "Sammys" running, not being quite sure what it is that makes them run except that all their neighbors are running, and they dare not stop lest they lose what is left of their self-respect. Three hundred years of American living has brought them freedom of worship, the right to vote, fine homes, the privilege to live in most neighborhoods, substantial bank accounts, and an exalted opinion of themselves, but not the opportunity to live in high destiny nor even a conviction of such destiny.

One may say what he wishes, but the fact remains that Jews in America are still victims of the haunting memories of the ghetto. The old beliefs are gone, yet not quite gone, for they remain to obsess most Jews. The beliefs are gone, but the Jews cannot quite escape them because, whether they like it or not, they drag after them the whole history of their family life, their group life, their four thousand-year-old heritage. These are the coiled springs that move them, and often they find themselves subconsciously dancing to ancient tunes.

No person can even begin to write a story like this alone; therefore I must record with deep gratitude the immeasurable assistance given me by so many individuals but without ascribing to them any responsibility for its content. I particularly wish to thank these friends and colleagues who have patiently given me personal comfort, fruitful suggestions, and technical aid: Dr. Vernon Wharton, Rabbi Jerome Mark, Mrs. Bolivar Lee Hait, Dr. Robert Brockway, Mrs. Mathe Allain, and Dr. Vincent Cassidy.

It is most important, moreover, to thank T. D. Larose, my non-Jewish brother-in-law and one of my favorite persons, for his profound suggestions about the Jewish family. I am inclined to believe that he has as good an insight into many aspects of the Jewish family as does the writer. Our wonderful, typically *yiddishe* mother-in-law, may her soul rest in peace, used to refer to him with deep affection as her *goishe kop*. (She spoke Yiddish with a Texas accent.) This is not necessarily a derogatory term; rather it means that such a person possesses a mentality which is fundamentally the mentality of a Christian, void of the peculiar inhibitions of a Jewish mind often twisted by the abnormalities of centuries of life in dispersion.

I am compelled to mention my appreciation to my uncle Abrasha, that lovable shoemaker-philosopher, a *chochom* (one who possesses knowledge, wisdom, and a sense of humor) if there ever was one, who used to read to me from Jewish writers when I was a child. His rich Yiddish speech was lyrical and intense, and he could make Sholem Aleichem's picture of shtetl life become real and exciting. Out of the past he was able to distill knowledge and experience, and voice a meaningful pattern of living. It was from him that I learned that life must not be taken for granted or carelessly thrown away but lived with completeness and grace. It was he, also, who got across to me the age-old truth, as he impressed upon me time and again, that a little philosophy will make a good Jew an unbeliever, whereas a great deal of philosophy will make of an unbeliever a good Jew.

Why does one undertake such a formidable task as this? Why does one spend years laboring, albeit it is a labor of love? Why does one study innumerable books and monographs by sociologists, anthropologists, historians, and read dozens and dozens of novels depicting Jewish life in nineteenth-century Eastern Europe and in modern America? Why pore over religious and philosophical material of various kinds and why consider so carefully the Bible, the Talmud, and a great many other writings on Judaism?

The answer is not simple. It has been said, half in jest and all in earnest, that a writer writes in about the same way an alcoholic drinks. His passion comes not from reason but from thirst. The big difference, however, is that the alcoholic hopes to lose himself in his bottle whereas the writer hopes to find himself in his manuscript. The writer, in part at least, writes to be with friends, although some of them are ghosts: the ghosts of Avrom, Moses, Isaiah, Job, and Micah, and the ghosts of those who were dragged to Babylon, and the ghosts who wandered through that medieval inferno known as Toledo, and the ghosts who walked the narrow, muddy streets of the shtetl, and the ghosts who starved in the miserable Warsaw ghetto, and the ghosts who still mourn over Buchenwald. It is also true that, in a very real sense, a writer writes to satisfy a basic selfish need, to understand himself, and finally to teach himself. Then there is the professional challenge, the sheer pleasure of discovery, and the feeling implied in the classic observation of the native of Nepal who climbed Mt. Everest simply because it was there. However, the most important reason as far as this writer is concerned is the one which would have been given by his grandfather—it is *beshert* (destined).

The writing of this story is both an inspiring and frightening experience. Indeed, it is as irrevocable as is my own family and more self-revealing than my strangest dream.

Contents

the
Jew and
His Family

I

I Will Make Thy Seed as the Dust of the Earth

Among the stories, legends, and fables in the Midrash—that rich source of homiletical commentary on Hebrew Scriptures—there is this passage (Genesis Rabbah) relating to the early background of the Jews:

As the dust of the earth extends from one end of the world to the other so your children will be scattered from one end of the world to the other. And as the dust of the earth can be blessed only through water, so Israel too can be blessed only in the virtue of the Torah, which is compared to water. And as the dust is made to be trampled on, so your children too will be made for kingdoms to trample on. And as dust wears vessels of metal away, but itself endures forever, so with Israel: All the idolatrous nations shall be naught but they shall endure.

Then they said unto him, "Tell us, we pray thee . . . ; What is thine occupation? and whence comest thou? . . . and of what people are thou?" And he said unto them, "I am a Hebrew; and I fear the Lord, the God of heaven, which hath made the sea and the dry land" (Jonah 1:8,9).

And it is written further, "Ye are my witness, saith the Lord, and my servant whom I have chosen: . . ." (Isaiah 43:10).

Indeed, *fregt di velt an alte kashe* (the world asks the same old question). Who are these eternal strangers? Where did they come

from? Where have they been and where are they going? What are
they doing here? And what is the nature of the belief to which they
have clung so tenaciously through the ages? When one considers
the great mass of commentary which has grown up about the Jews
and their religion, it is surprising how little they are understood. The
Jewish story remains, after four thousand years, somewhat of a puz-
zle to historians, anthropologists, and sociologists. The Jews have
indeed challenged an axiom, for according to all laws of social science they should have become extinct long ago, just as so many
other social groups have been snuffed out throughout history. To
be sure, much investigation has been done regarding Judaism, but
we still know too little to speak confidently or with a sense of finality
about it. Those who have explained it have suddenly found themselves confronted with Lord Byron's query: "Who will then explain
the explanation?"

Throughout the centuries there must have been many Chaldeans,
Egyptians, Babylonians, Greeks, Romans, Christians as well as Jews,
who wished that somewhere along the way God had broken the spell
of silence concerning the strange phenomenon that is the Jew. Since
time immemorial people have asked their oracles, witch doctors,
wizards, soothsayers, their priests, sages, historians, and psychologists, whatever be their level of civilization, to explain the nature
and meaning of this unique group. The only common conclusion all
these sources of wisdom could reach is that "Jews are people who
think otherwise." And what has been the result—only that they
continued to be hated, feared, and, yes, even needed.

From Nebuchadnezzar to Nicolae Nicolaevich, from the Roman
legions to the Nazi supermen there have been efforts to destroy them.
Yes, even further back, for did not Pharoah Mernepath (*ca.* 1225
B.C.) cut deeply into a piece of granite these words: "Israel is deso-
late, her seed is no more"? Yet these giants have been covered by
the sands of time or the rubble of their wars, and the Jews have remained, single-minded and conscientious, sometimes forgotten by the
world, sometimes remembered, sometimes flattered, sometimes in-

sulted, their religious ideal reflected in the mirror of the soul and their story an episode without a beginning and without an ending.

Indeed, it is impossible to perceive the panorama of their entire experience in its four-thousand-year-old perspective without realizing that it is one of the most stupendous and inexplicable triumphs of the human mind and spirit. And so the shadow of their collective spirit continues to wander on in the wilderness of modern life as though guided by some invisible hand. Each person, each family, each group has a history of its own, a private and often secret diary. No outsider can read it. Likewise, no one can recall any other person's memories; if he perishes, his memories perish with him, as when a group perishes its memories are lost forever. In analyzing the fabric of Judaism it quickly becomes evident that for thousands of years Jews have somehow been able to hold on to their memories as individuals and as a group, each one wearing a tough outer shell which contained the fruition of the past and the dreams of the future, and which protected them from outside pressures. This containment kept them from wandering away and brought them continuity equal to no other in the history of men.

That a knowledge of the past is necessary for an understanding of the present and as a guide for the future is agreed upon by most intelligent people. Thus it is that if we hope to penetrate, even in a small measure, the inner substance of the Jewish soul, where their secret really lies, it will be imperative to glance into the history of the Jews, although it should be made clear at the outset that the history of the development of Judaism does not lend itself to any common measure. This does seem certain, in this connection: the ordinary yardsticks appear to be piffling and irrelevant.

For the Jews history and Judaism cannot be separated, because the relation of God and man to each other gives meaning to history, and history gives meaning to their relationship. And Jews are convinced that it was they who first crystallized the idea of the one true God. This is why the history of the Jews resembles a wave starting in the middle of the ocean, never at rest, moody at times, calm at other times, stormy, sometimes confident, sometimes weak, flinging a challenge at everything and everybody it meets. Interestingly enough, in Jewish thought the universal struggle is not between man and his environment, not between good and evil, light and darkness, not even between God and the Devil, but rather between God and the human creatures "He created in his own image."

In the final analysis it may be said that the Jewish story concerns itself with the confrontation of a strange group of people and their unique God, and with both of these lining up against the world.

Despite the fact that the entire religion of the Jews consists basically of their passionate love of God and that their *raison d'etre* is to be in the right relation to Him, there were times in their history when they believed He was pleased to have His jest with His people.

To be sure, He chose them as His own but He has been trying them ever since. Long ago they got the feeling that Yahveh was a thoroughly human God. He made mistakes of which *Homo sapiens* is probably the worst. He was often kind and gracious, forgiving and forgetting. At other times He was vengeful, bloodthirsty, and difficult. At times He talked too much and at other times He would say nothing at all. Sometimes He would show Himself but at other times He would hide Himself. He caused the death of all the firstborn in Egypt. Yet He suggested that one should take a drink of wine to gladden his heart. He was also very jealous; He asked in the first commandment that He be placed above all the rest of the gods. He must have been first a little forgetful, too, for in listing the ten basic elements of human behavior He left out the greatest of all commandments. It occurs in Leviticus 19:18 and reads very simply: "Thou shalt love thy neighbor as thyself."

Because of these characteristics Jews have often taken issue with their God. However, it must be said that most of the time it was, and still is, essentially a case of bargaining with Him. "I'll give you my soul if you will give me your blessing!"

And what was God's answer to all this bickering? It is given in Psalms 46:10: "Be still, and know that I am God: I will be exalted among the heathen, I will be exalted in the earth." Nevertheless they continued to disagree. There was Avrom who argued with Him about

Sodom. There was Jacob who wrestled with His angel and would not let go until he got what he wanted. There was Moses who disobeyed Him and there was Job who questioned Him. There have always been the Jewish women who never quite forgave Him for putting them in the same category with cattle and real estate in the tenth commandment. And then there was Bontzye Schweig who embarrassed Him.[1]

The story of Bontzye Schweig is a graphic example of the early Jew's attitude about his relationship with God. It is a most engaging tale, human, touching, simple, yet it contains the very magic calculated to startle one's soul into new motivation.

Bontzye Schweig (the silent) was a poor, unimportant little man who lived miserably and died miserably in his poor, unimportant little shtetl, unnoticed by anyone. His was "a quiet birth, a quiet life, a quiet death and a quieter burial." However in the other world things were different. When Bontzye was brought up before the heavenly host for his eternal judgment it was soon discovered that Bontzye had been a good man, no more no less, simply a good man, and the Judge of the universe, blessed be His name, offered Bontzye his reward. What reward?

"Anything! Take what you will. Everything is yours."

Bontzye could not believe his ears.

"Taki! really?" he asked.

"Taki, taki, taki," came the answer from all ends.

And Bontzye smiled and said, "I would like to have every day, for breakfast, a hot roll with fresh butter." And the heavenly court all looked down a little ashamed.

Martin Buber sums all this up very well when he says: "Thus the whole history of the world, the hidden, real world history, is a dialogue between God and His creatures; a dialogue in which man is a true, legitimate partner, who is entitled and empowered to speak his own independent word out of his own being."[2]

[1] Isaac Leib Peretz, *Stories and Pictures* (Philadelphia: Jewish Publication Society, 1906), 171.

[2] Martin Buber, *Israel and the World* (New York: Schocken Books, 1963), 16.

According to Jewish history God revealed Himself through His actions, from the vision of Avrom in the dim past when He first made Himself known, to the binding *B'nai B'rith* set up at the foot of thunderous Mt. Sinai; from the settlement in Canaan, the first real homeland of the Jews, to the Davidic era when they first became a nation; from the exile into Babylon, when the Jewish group ceased to exist as a going concern, to its rebirth from that experience with new spiritual strength and a new Talmud as their guide; from the dispersion throughout the world, to the miracle of the re-establishment of the state of Israel as a homeland. All this time the Jew was "despised and rejected of men, a man of sorrows and acquainted with grief: . . ." (Isaiah 53:3), yet inspired by God's assurance that "ye shall be unto me a kingdom of priests, and a holy nation" (Exod. 19:6).

They wandered from place to place, from people to people, their spirits providing them with passports, as though some giant force were driving them on, as indeed there must have been, "for thou shalt go to all that I shall send thee, and whatsoever I command thee, thou shalt speak. Be not afraid because of them" (Jer. 1:6).

To be sure, they did not go alone, for "the Lord went before them by day in a pillar of a cloud, to lead them the way; and by night in a pillar of fire, . . ." (Exod. 13:21). Sometimes they were victorious and at other times they failed miserably, but like the phoenix they seemed to be able to rise from their own ashes. Indeed, they listened and went and felt Yahveh touch their lives with some mysterious, transfiguring element, perhaps His glory.

In their moments of truth they believed that they were implements of history, that their ideals could prove to be the hinge of fate which would ultimately turn and, turning, would hurl them into a world of decency, justice, and one God, for did He not say, "in thee shall all the nations be blessed." But they also realized that they were lonely; this is inevitable, for the ways of the iconoclast are rarely pleasant, the breaking of idols is certain to wound many souls.

In the story of mankind there have been no people as lonely over so long a time as the Jews. Avrom stood alone when, in a momentary glance, he looked into eternity. It was a lonely Moses, strolling with his flock, whom the burning bush called. Isaiah, walking alone in the wilderness, told the world that nations are but specks of sand when compared to God's majesty and infinity. Micah was alone when he admonished mankind to do justly, love mercy, and walk humbly with God. Hosea stood alone when he taught that Yahveh was not a God of vengeance or war, but a God of justice and love. There was David as he stood alone against the mighty Goliath. There was the Jewish slave who went alone when Titus (whom the Romans called "*Benefactor generis humani*," "Benefactor of the human race") dragged him to Rome and had special coins struck bearing the figure of a woman in chains, with the following inscription: *Judea capta, Judea devicta*—Judah the captive, Judah the vanquished. And then there was the branded Jew who walked alone to the crematorium in Dachau quietly saying his *Shema* and knowing full well that the truth of God is mercy, peace, and loving kindness and the commitment to a life that, in itself, is a triumph over death.

They were all lonely, but they also shared a comradeship with each other and with all mankind, because they all had in common one everlasting God whose face they could not see but whose "glory they saw as it passeth by." They were lonely, yet their loneliness was never that of the self-centered or the frustrated or the cynical whose sense of isolation is often embittered by resentment. The isolation of the idealist, the visionary, and the courageous one knows no anger or resentment, for he is convinced that he lives with the imperishable. Oddly enough, it was this loneliness which helped to nourish the spirits of the Jews and give direction to their power, enabling them to make one of the greatest discoveries of all time. They discovered not new seas, mountains, continents, or even new stars but new levels of living, new realms of achievement, new areas of hope, and new dreams for men to follow.

The Jewish people simply cannot be fitted into any known sociological, anthropological, or historical category. They constitute a minority by virtue of their historical experience, religion, style of living, and geographical background. C. Bezalel Sherman observes that "Jews defy categorization as an entity. Are they a religious fellowship, an historical continuum, a cultural group with peculiar racial traits, or a people? They would seem to be all these and more."[3] When Balaam pronounced a blessing upon the children of Israel he said: "Lo, it is a people that shall live alone, and shall not be reckoned among the nations." And Philo, the philosopher, added that Israel shall be apart by reason of the pecularities of their customs; they will not mix with other people so that they may not deviate from their special way of life. The writer's pious grandfather—*alev asholom* (may he rest in peace)—would have answered this perplexing issue simply by saying, "Israel was chosen." His sociologically oriented grandchild says only that here is revealed the creative genius of a people. Neither answer is completely satisfying, for no creation of the spirit can be completely explained.

This predicament has proved to be a two-edged sword for the Jews. On the one hand their inability to fit into a category has resulted in embarrassment at least and in misery at most. On the other hand it has given Judaism the uniqueness without which it could never have survived. Throughout most of their history, until very recently, Jews were quite certain that they did fit into a category; they were God's chosen for better or worse. They believed their covenant with God placed them in a very special category, for it is written, "Ye are the children of the living God" (Hos. 1:10), and by means of the extraordinary strength generated from this category they have been preserved unbroken through generation after generation.

Indeed, the Jews as a group may not lend themselves to social scientific analysis, but they were lusty and vigorous before Babylon and Nineveh built their monuments, they were learned before Rameses cut his hieroglyphics, they were skilled architects before the Pharoahs dreamed of erecting pyramids, they were warriors before the Greeks captured Troy, they had cities before Rome was built, they had poets before Homer sang his songs, they believed in one

---

[3] C. Bezalel Sherman, *The Jew Within American Society* (Detroit: Wayne University Press, 1961), vi.

God before the coming of the Christian Master. Their children were taught to read from the Torah before the Latin alphabet had reached its final form, long before Cyrillus and Methodius had given writing to the Slavs and before Runic characters were known to the Germans of the north.

Had the Jews been devoted to an unchangeable priestly religion they would never have flourished. Had they been a nation they would never have survived. Had they been a race, they might have long ago lost their identity. But the Jews were more than these. At the heart of Jewish life was the cult of the family, the rule of the Torah, and the guidance of the Lord Himself. With those elements they built a wall around themselves and still remain to this day to disturb each other and the world at large.

Perhaps God was unfair to the Jews. By creating immortal ideas in their beings, by implanting in them dreams and visions so difficult to achieve, by giving them sensitive imaginations to haunt them, by hypnotizing them with the "chosen people" notion to drive them on, and by eternally dangling before them their divine purpose in the universe, He has made them plastic and fluid in His hands and has given them a dowry which may prove fatal.

Indeed, God's dealing with the Jews appears to be either a case of the most malicious irony or a splendid promise of fulfillment. Only time, a great deal of time, can answer the riddle, for it is written: "The life of man is numbered by days (but) the days of Israel are innumerable."

In an effort to isolate the universals that underlie the nature, shape, and content of Judaism it is first necessary to put on what the sociologist Vilfredo Pareto called "cultural lenses," in this case the cultural lenses of Judaism. Most non-Jews lack the special insight necessary for an understanding of the peculiarities typical to Jews. They lack the proper frame of mind, and no matter how they try, they can go so far and no farther in comprehending the Jewish ideal. Indeed, the source of Judaism may be hidden from most of us, yet it speaks with great authority and persuasion. This is an observation beyond dispute and upon which too great an emphasis cannot be placed.

One quality which has always impressed observers of the Jewish scene has been the belief firmly fixed in the consciousness of the average Jew that there is but one God, Lord of the Universe, and that His Torah and His way of life are destined to bring decency, peace, and goodwill not only to Jews but to all mankind. Sometimes naively, sometimes arrogantly, sometimes irritatingly, but always enthusiastically Jews have asserted for four thousand years their confidence in their credo, in their *raison d'etre*, and have maintained their optimism about their worth and destiny in terms often unacceptable to most people. Yet this has been the force to which the Jewish ideal has been dedicated, the wellspring, sometimes running like a subterranean stream, sometimes covering the land like a flood, from which they have drawn their ethics and their sense of values, their courage and their faith. It is this faith which is the key to their survival—a faith which maintains that along with man's hatred, greed, ugliness, sadism there is also a subconscious sense that life is better than death, that love is better than hate, that creation is better than annihilation, and that under every No in life there must also be a Yes. The result has been, at least up to the present, that what the Jews have believed so faithfully they have achieved against unbelievable odds. Their religious experiences have been, in a sense, like the rays of the sun—boundless, shooting upward and downward, without circumference, the center being their God and the pattern for this being their religion known as Judaism.

It has been argued that religion is nothing more than a concealed desire to escape from the mad confusion of life, the cruel injustices, the feverish strife, and that the thoughts of peace, eternity, and God are merely veiled longings for death, the consoling vision of the fugitive from existence. And Jung would have us believe that God does not exist for Himself, that He is merely a psychic phenomenon, and that divine action arises from one's own inner self.

Yet a belief in a Supreme Being must have existed since the beginning of men. Men have looked at the wonders and mystery of the starry sky, the falling rain, the thunder and lightning, the changing seasons, the sprouting seed, and the growing child, at birth and death, and they realized there must be a greater power than themselves. Religion has survived for so long and has played so vital a part in the lives of human beings that we cannot pass it by.

This may be said with certainty: religion is man's effort to interpret the supernatural, to appease it in order to get its help in coming to terms with his environment. It is that which he must lean on because he is too frail to stand alone; it is that which is beyond his campfire. Every human being needs an anchorage, something on which he must depend for security. Man, being a finite creature, requires many fixed points of reference, stable foci, or centers of gravity in his everyday living in order to have a sense of stability and well-being. Religion is one of the basics of those focal points of orientation. In short, the purpose of religion is to create a bulwark against inner and outer chaos in order to make life bearable for the individual and to aid the group to survive.

To be sure, one of the serious weaknesses in man's religious outlook and his definition of it, one which has brought untold misery, is that each man seeks a deity after his own heart and his God is thus his ideal. Spinoza once said that a community of triangles would worship a triangular God. And Walter Bagehot, in his essay "Ignorance of Man," puts it very succinctly:

> The Ethiopean Gods have Ethiopean lips,
> Bronze cheeks and wooly hair;
> The Grecian Gods are like the Greeks,
> Or keen-eyed, cold, and fair.

The writer's saintly grandfather, who had never been beyond a few miles from his shtetl, would have given as a definition of religion one as narrow and parochial in outlook and comparable in perspective to that given by Mr. Thwackum in Fielding's novel *Tom Jones* who said: "When I mention religion I mean the Christian religion: and not only the Christian religion but the Protestant religion; and not only the Protestant religion but the church of England." He would have said simply that religion is Judaism: and not only Judaism but

Orthodox Judaism; and not only Orthodox Judaism but the particular Judaism of his shtetl.

Philosophers agree that the human mind can penetrate to the most hidden recesses of the universe, but they also agree that the human mind reaches a point beyond which it simply cannot go. At this point it must turn to another "system" which we call the spirit. That is the system which can prove to be a creative force more powerful, more profound, and more meaningful than all man's accumulated knowledge, and which can lead to a higher and more desirable world, reveal for him new horizons, and offer him a new purpose in life. The spirit can do this because it can help liberate men from the chains of selfish desires and because it concerns itself with thoughts, feelings, and inspirations beyond the physical and the sensate.

There is an object lesson to be learned from this particular issue in life. Science and philosophy were born under different stars and are equally incapable of seeing the same things as significant, meaningful, or worthwhile. Most scientists are inclined to believe that philosophers deal only in opinions and value judgments for which they can offer no empirical proof. But then how does one define the undefinable or measure the unmeasurable? An excellent example of man's effort to give utterance to that which is really unutterable, to grasp the strength and beauty, the remoteness and meaning of God may be found in the 139th Psalm. In other pages of the Bible, God generally speaks to man, but here men speak to God and their own hearts. Here is a splendid illustration of the confessional *par excellence*, a demonstration of the basic principle of psychotherapy, and a moving reflection of the loneliness of the human spirit.

Thus it was that about four thousand years ago a vague new idea came up out of the mists of unrecorded time and uncharted space and settled in the consciousness of a small group of Hebrews wandering around in the desert.[4] An idea which brought with it an immense

---

[4] It is interesting to note that first the name "Jacob" was changed to "Israel." In Genesis 33:20 Jacob erected an altar which he called *El-Elohe-Israel*, that is, "God, the God of Israel," and it was much later that the Hebrews became known as the "Israelites" from the term *Yisroel* which means "the man who sees God" (I Sam. 13:6).

sensibility, a keen desire to seek the inner meaning and the laws of men's conduct, the truth about their existence, and the awareness that such meaning, laws, and truth are their responsibilities. Here was a tremendous step in the crystallization of the spirit. And where do we search for the genesis of this mystery, where are its roots, where the fountainhead of this idea? Physics, chemistry, mathematics know nothing of this matter. Even history, anthropology, and sociology are to a large extent silent. The answer is, of course, that it was no one less than the God of all Gods. And so from the darkness of Mesopotamian paganism, from the terrors of Egyptian magic, from the mysterious *gnosis* of Babylonian thinking, and from the fortune telling of the Greeks came at last Yahveh.

Immediately the Jews fell into His hands, which is both a fearful and wondrous thing—fearful because one who falls into the hands of God may be "despised and rejected," wondrous because he is "God's first born" and holy for "I am holy." The fact of the matter is that the Jews had no choice in this arrangement. They needed a road map of the universe, a guide to the guarantor of the order of things, and this was the only way to get it.

From then on their business was with eternity. *En Berayrah*—there is no choice—that was their secret weapon in the shtetl, and it is their secret weapon today. Indeed, whereas logic demands the universal, Jews have ever supplied the particular, the novel, the unexpected. Perhaps that is why George Bernard Shaw said of them: "The Jew is born civilized."

So the Jews made a bargain with Yahveh the untouchable, the incomprehensible, the indescribable. They picked Him as their God above all others and promised to fear Him, to follow all His commandments, and to say of Him eternally: "*Shema Yisroel: Adonoi Elohanu, Adonoi Echod*"—"Hear, O Israel: The Lord our God, the Lord is one." He in turn promised them that "If ye will hearken unto my voice . . . ye shall be mine own treasure from the nations and ye shall be unto me a kingdom of priests and a holy nation." And He promised further to reveal to them His majestic truth to be known as the Torah.[5] And he would bless them with a succession of great leaders who, in sheer courage, social passion, and spiritual insight, would outrank all others and continue to this day as beacons of light to all nations.

Thus emerged the concept of monotheism into the sunlight. It is, of course, naive for any of us to believe that the idea originated with Avrom, or any other one person or group of persons in any one place or during any one age. It is an idea which developed slowly and painfully among many peoples in many places over many years. However, it must be admitted that the Jews did help congeal the idea and spread it far and wide. Monotheism did crystallize the principle of unity of mankind: one "Judge of all the earth," (Gen. 18:25) with "one law" for all (Num. 15:15, 16 and Isaiah 42:4).

Inspired by the glorious uniqueness of their relationship with the one God and believing Him to be sovereign and supreme, they sealed the bargain with an everlasting covenant to which there was one reservation: "For my thoughts are not your thoughts, neither are your ways my ways, saith the Lord. For as the heavens are higher than the earth, so are my ways higher than your ways, and my thoughts than your thoughts" (Isaiah 55:8, 9). Nevertheless they accepted His Torah as the source of their theology and the guide to their life, thus getting in one package a religious philosophy and a pattern of living both emphasizing not only wisdom but action. Here then was their sacred literature, their road map to the universe, and perhaps a plan for a human community not yet built and a way of life not yet lived.

History records many judgments, judgments made by individuals and by nations, but the judgment of those primitive Hebrews in accepting God and His Torah was a promise of accomplishment incomparable, of an experience in life and its wonders such as few people have ever known. It was, in effect, a decision to lead the world, not in matters of political conquests, in the pride of military might, in

---

[5] There is a legend in the Talmud which tells how the Torah was refused by various nations in turn because of the stringent demand it made on them. Small wonder Jews sometimes seem arrogant about their "yoke."

the development of industry, but in the matters of the spirit and the mind. It was a promise to the world in the words of Ezekiel (34:16): "I will seek that which was lost, and will bring again that which was driven away, and will bind up that which was broken and will strengthen that which was sick: . . ."

Cultures are not born with human beings but are found in museums, in libraries, and particularly in the written word. From the ancient papyrus roll to the modern microfilm, man has depended on the written word to store his accumulated knowledge and wisdom for use by generations to come. The foundation of the storehouse of the Judaic structure is the written word in the Torah—all other words are merely commentary.

To be sure, Judaism did not develop without syncretism. Throughout history the Jews have borrowed from the Mesopotamians, the Canaanites, the Babylonians, the Greeks, and many others. It is well to note they generally borrowed only those ideas and practices which seemed consistent with their own.

Jewish legend has it that when God began His program of creation He created first of all the Torah, which was written with black fire on white fire, and which He kept on His lap. Furthermore, when He got around to the business of creating the world He took counsel with the Torah, which, incidentally, was skeptical about the value of an earthly world in the first place.

Jews have no monuments of metal and stone as do most other groups. Their one great monument is the Torah. This and a few other frail symbols—the candelabra, the star of David, the ark, and the altar—have called forth in them great faith and hope, strength and courage.

Despite their strong feeling about the Torah and its meaning in their lives and destiny, Jews long ago sensed the danger in following dogma too closely. They realized there is only one thing about which man may be truly dogmatic—that there is no such thing as a dogma. Martin Buber puts it ably when he states that "in the religious life of Judaism, primary importance is not given to dogma but to the remembrance and the expectation of a concrete situation: the encoun-

ter of God and men."[6] To help them unravel single threads of the
Judaic fabric in order to adjust to changing situations, there developed in the lives of Jews a book of commentary on the Torah called
the Talmud. The Talmud is the body of Jewish law and legend as
expounded in the Jewish academies of Palestine and Babylon and is
considered to be the generic designation of the whole of early rabbinic
literature. It is not a dual treatise, but appeals to the imagination and
the feelings and to all that is noble. Its basic theme has always been
the equality of men, and it was meant to serve all humanity. When
Jews became perplexed it was their guide.

Jews submitted to the talmudic voice because they realized that
their very existence depended upon it. It was the source of life, the
teacher, the guide, the counselor; it was the model of justice, truth,
wisdom, and spiritual strength.

Because we become the things we love, Yahveh, the Torah, and
the Talmud all set their indelible stamp on Jewish life. In time a
substantial body of thought, customs, and institutions developed,
slowly, even painfully, modified by surrounding pressures. In time
this pattern of thinking led to the formation of a people—a society
based on this common ground—and produced a special type of character among Jews.

The question "What kind of people are the Jews?" inevitably takes
precedence over any particular question of sociology, anthropology,
philosophy, psychology, and even religion, but the question cannot
be separated from the elements that give rise to such questions. What
are the ingredients of the Jewish character? Despite the fact that
character is intangible and unique, it is neither abstract nor isolated;
it is yet both cause and effect, creation and creator. It is the product
of a thousand factors of history, geography, various cultures, unique
experiences, physiological predispositions, and a thousand yesterdays
and yesteryears; and it influences, in turn, the manifestations of these
factors. What kind of people, then, are the Jews? What have they
inherited and what have they created? What values do they cherish

[6] Buber, *Israel and the World,* 14.

and what standards do they maintain? What fears do they confess and what hopes do they dream about? What are their motivating interests, sentiments, and passions, and finally what is their *raison d'etre*? How do they view themselves and how do they view others? This remains certain: Judaism has fused its human ingredients into something approaching a type, and students of history, sociology, and psychology tend to confirm the conclusion that, somehow, this type has been largely responsible for the survival of the group.

The Jewish character, then, is an amalgam of inheritance, environment, and experience. The inheritance is basically biblical Judaism and Greek philosophy; the environment, like the inheritance, has been varied both in time and space, for Jews have lived in many different lands and times; the experience, viewed from first to last, seems to have been all movement and energy. It has been one of a struggle for existence, physical, spiritual, and cultural, in a tangle of centuries, a struggle emanating as it did from the tension between the awareness of the reality all around them and their drive for the dream of the future, which has demanded of Jews that they develop an apocalyptic literature, a particular social philosophy, and a unique style of living. Together these gave rise to their conception of man, his duty, and his destiny, which in turn defined the basic elements on which civilized living is based: justice, righteousness, freedom, and democracy.

Being a Jew cuts across all other boundaries. You are no longer a professional or a laborer, no longer rich or poor, American or Polish, Democrat or Republican. You are not for Johnson or Goldwater, you are first of all a Jew. There is a world kinship in this category comparable to no other, yet it is not without its pain and misery. The consciousness of possessing a world of their own and a binding as well as demanding spiritual and cultural kinship system has helped the Jews find peace, solitude, and an indestructible inner security. Yet it has also made of them a pariah people, distrusted, pitied, hunted, frustrated, often suffering from humiliation, fear, and deep anger at injustice. It has then made them want to "die all the time and they keep on living all the time."[7] Obviously this is not a wholesome condition. Jews are an example *par excellence* of ambivalence regarding themselves which is quite understandable. It is as though the powers of the earth have conspired to exterminate them; yet, as they look about them, it becomes evident also that the superhuman endurance of the group must testify that along the way it must have talked with and walked with some superhuman authority. On the one hand, Jews want very much to live up to the dignity, grandeur, and importance which they believe God expects of them, while, on the other hand, there are times in their lives when they feel a weariness and fatigue, times of inner loneliness, and deep hurt.

It is indeed ironical that it is the dictum of Nietzsche, who was the progenitor of Hitler's philosophy of hate and destruction, which gives a clue to the solution of the psychic dilemma faced by the Jews: "He who has the *why* to live can bear with almost any *how*."

That social circumstances do profoundly modify human behavior appears to be a truism accepted by most students of human behavior. The attempt to fulfill their psychic needs and to manage their social conflicts with greater artistry, became the matrix of the Jew's personal sanity, balance, and security. No matter what society, men and women must ever face the purely personal and profoundly individual issues of love and hate, status and motivation, life and death with a certain type of preparation which results in a certain type of wisdom. In their history the Jews have earned this wisdom the hard way, the light of one generation kindling the one to follow. It has proved to be the brilliant cloud which guided them in the ancient wilderness and the pillar of fire which illumined their way in the modern Diaspora. And finally it has jelled into a group individuality, an ethnic psychological group with a distinct style of living, with particular tastes, predispositions, inclinations, memories, loyalties, and aspirations.

Jews simply have to be this way and they have to live this way.

[7] Isaac B. Singer, *Commentary*, XXXVI (1963), 364–72.

Here again it is a case of "en berayrah." There is a most prophetic and memorable tale told in the Talmud which makes this point frightfully meaningful not only for Jews but for all men. Once a Roman authority issued a decree that Jews might no longer study the Torah; however, Rabbi Akiba continued to teach not only the knowledge of the Torah but love for that knowledge. A friend of the Rabbi said to him: "Rabbi, are you not afraid, you must know that what you are doing will bring you great danger." The Rabbi answered, "Let me tell you a story which will explain my position in the matter. A fox was walking near a stream one day and in the water he saw many fish swimming about. Said the fox to the fish 'Why do you rush about so?' 'We rush about,' they answered, 'because we are afraid of the fisherman's net.' 'Come up on dry land,' said the fox, 'and live with me in safety.' But the fish said, 'You do not speak like the wise animal you are. If we are not safe in the water which is our natural home, how much less safe shall we be on land where we must surely die.' " "It is exactly so with us Jews," continued the Rabbi. "The Torah is our life and length of days. We may, while loving and studying the Torah, be in great danger from our enemies, but if we were to give it up, we would surely disappear and be no more."

The overwhelming central fact of this story projects itself at every turn. It was from their assumptions and traditions, their ideals and goals, their fantasy, legendry, poetry, and symbolism that individual Jews have, in the past, gained the lofty image of themselves as well as the God-given uniqueness of the entire group. This complex of ideas has fostered the belief that the Jew is a person who is in the right fellowship with God, his basic credo, his neighbor, his fellow man, himself, and the world in general; that he is in focus, in tune with the basic facts of life; and that the stature of his personality will be dwarfed or expanded by the amount of interest and concern he has in these matters. And finally Jews have gained the steadfast conviction that throughout all time it has been their choice and responsibility, one and all, to climb from the dust of the feet to the spirit of the mountain, and to become an *am olam*—an eternal people.

Where and when did this terrible yet magnificent experience begin? Where and when was the mold created which shaped the substance of the Jewish soul? Where and when was it said by them: "My times are in your hand"? It was in the Haran desert, it was when God took a hand in man's history, it was the drama enacted by Avrom once upon a certain time.

II

Lift Up Thine Eyes and Look

And it came to pass that Terah of the line of Shem left Ur of Chaldea and took with him his son Avrom and Avrom's wife Sara, who was also his half-sister, being the daughter of Terah's favorite concubine Shelomite, and Lot, Terah's grandson, and they all turned toward Haran to the north, for it had been said to them: "Prepare ye a way through the desert for God."

Here, then, begins a fabulous story, one which explodes in images, fantasies, manifestoes, and pronouncements—a story calculated to sweep the reader back in time and forward in judgment.

There are moments in history which transcend time and take on an ageless meaning. Such a moment in Jewish history came to Avrom in the Haran desert, for there he found himself in the midst of creating a fabric of human destiny. There the drama of Yahveh began to unfold, there the fulcrum was fixed upon which the world took an unexpected turn and revealed a hidden portion of itself never before quite grasped by the human mind; there a flame was set which has never quite ceased to burn during all these uncounted generations and which has leaped from century to century, from continent to continent. There it was pledged to Avrom: "I will bless those who bless you and curse those who curse you"; there Avrom received the assurance: "Fear not for I am your shield"; there Avrom was ad-

monished: "Not by might nor by power, but by my spirit, saith the
Lord." There Avrom was commanded: "I am the first and I am the
last, and beside me there is no God"; and there Avrom was blessed:
"The Lord make his face to shine upon thee and be gracious unto
thee: The Lord lift up his countenance upon thee and give thee
peace." There Avrom gained immortality in one brief hour. Indeed,
there was a promise which would set the world in motion, and there
the foundation was laid for all future Judaism.

To be sure, Avrom is one of the most commanding figures in the
Bible. He must have possessed deep humility, strong faith, and much
courage. His experience was one of those truly rare in the annals
of mankind, high in poetic beauty, boldness, and daring. He molded
into a pattern of living a spirit of freedom, a sense of justice, a belief
in humanity couched in *divre shalom we-emeth* (words of peace and
truth).

It is generally believed that the mainstream of Judaism begins
with Moses at Sinai but there must have been things resembling a
Torah and a Talmud long before that time. To be sure, many changes
have occurred in the theological and philosophical thinking of the
Jews from the early contemplations to the modern Jewish sages, from
Avrom of Ur to Martin Buber of Israel.

The entire story of Avrom presents a question of appealing puzzle-
ment. It is impossible to ignore this vague figure in the stream of
religious events or to escape the finger which history has been point-
ing at him for four thousand years. Whatever road one travels in
the realm of man's social and moral achievement he inevitably comes
at last upon the austere figure of Avrom. Here was a person who
attacked the very foundation of the primitive world with its multi-
tude of gods prancing through a charade as so many wooden puppets,
substituting for it at least the germ of a new spiritual and moral outlook wholly alien and antagonistic to most of mankind of his time
(as well as to most of mankind even today). Say what one will,
Avrom is a genuinely historic figure.[1]

[1] Some four thousand years ago, the Sumerians set down in writing their con-

As literary history the story of Avrom is of little significance. Of necessity any portrayal of Avrom—and it must be a portrait rather than a biography—must seem kaleidoscopic. Fragments of fact and conjecture fall into a colorful pattern which, in turn, stimulates the imagination. Yet one cannot escape the feeling that the basic elements are there. What is really important about this whole story is what it has to say to mankind.

There is a great mixture of the personal and the subjective in the telling of the tale of Avrom. If one is to look for the essence of Avrom's experience one cannot but search within himself. For such a treatment as is here undertaken has deep personal interest and dramatic personal appeal, and unless one experiences this interest and this appeal in one's self one can hardly communicate them to others. No matter the hows and whys of this tale, this remains certain: the spinning wheel of the ages has spun much fact and fancy about this person, part deity, part mystic, and part man. And the mystery that surrounds the story of Avrom is as inexplicable today as it must have been in the time of the early Hebrews. Surely no fiction can be stranger than the juxtaposition of these facts—the ones recording the events of Avrom's earthly life, his gravitation to Yahveh, and his influence on all human history.

Many people may question the capacity of the one man to create such a tremendous idea. In reality one cannot conceive of him as one person but rather as a procession of persons.

The desert that day seemed like a day of judgment. That day Avrom went into the sanctuary of God and caught a glimpse of His glory. That day Avrom grasped the First Cause.

The heat was so intense that it radiated like waves in all directions as though it were the ebb and flow of a tide pressing down on one with a great weight; and there reigned over the landscape a vast

ception of how their riverbound world was created, recording a myth that was ancient even at that time. The story is echoed in the first chapter of Genesis, for the Hebrew writers almost certainly derived their idea of creation, like those of the Garden of Eden, the Deluge, and other traditional Old Testament stories, from the "Land Between the Rivers."

silence. Each sand dune was filled with hidden mysteries as well as with painful cruelties. Indeed, in the desert there exists a strange paradox for here there is a freedom found in no other place, yet here one resigns himself to an inexplicable sort of servility.

All that day Avrom and his family had been moving slowly toward the distant hills near Haran. They felt an unusual weariness, for the desert can stun and fascinate one with its golden and purple hues and can strangle and burn one with its sweltering heat and ever-blowing wind. There is a bewitching beauty about it all, but a beauty which is torturously deceptive.

The pattering of donkey hooves had been like water dripping from a rock making rhythmic sounds, remote and soothing to Avrom's ears. Often during the day Avrom had felt drowsy, yet ever so often bits of his past life kept flashing before his eyes, vivid and exciting, as though they all happened yesterday. He could not only see clearly but he could also taste, smell, and hear life in Ur, the capital city of the Sumerians (one of the oldest cultures of Mesopotamia and the center of life in the entire Akkadian country).

Avrom chuckled to himself as he recalled his mother's telling him the legend of his birth and early life. He knew it was not true, but he loved to listen to the story again and again, because he loved his mother's other fairy tales and her songs about the moon goddess Sin. The night Avrom was born, went the legend, an enormous comet came up from the eastern horizon and swallowed up four giant stars each fixed in a different quarter of heaven. The astrologers immediately recognized the sign and concluded that Avrom would be a mighty emperor, that his descendants would multiply like the stars in the heavens, inherit the earth for all eternity, dethroning kings and taking over their lands. When King Nimrod heard about this he sent for Terah and offered to buy the infant so that he might destroy him. Terah had no choice but to agree. However, unknown to Nimrod, Terah submitted a slave woman's son for his own. Then Terah hid Avrom in a cave across the river, and God Himself cared for him during the next ten years. When Avrom came out of the cave "he spoke the Holy tongue of Hebrew, despised the sacred groves, loathed idols, and trusted in the strength of his creation."[2]

Again and again Avrom tried to break the spell which gripped him but he could not. If his group could only reach those purple hills in the shimmering distance, there, somehow, one might get beyond the desert, beyond the earth, the sky, perhaps even beyond life itself. "It is a strange thing," mused Avrom, "how there is ever the hint of revelation among the hills." Man has ever found help and healing in the hills, for the hills possess the things that most men long for and need. "I lift up my eyes to the hills from whence cometh my help," he has said throughout the ages. Indeed, measured against the life of the hills a man's life is but a brief moment, yet as their purple shadows fall across a thousand generations they say to every man in a mysterious voice that permanence is possible for those who have the strength, the courage, and the wisdom; for they "who wait upon the Lord shall mount up with wings as eagles, they shall run and not be weary, and they shall walk and not faint." If he could only stand face to face with those hills, those lasting, exalted hills, he would feel so much stronger.

He recalled vividly and painfully a night in another desert near Ur across the Euphrates when he had run away from home; the stars were bright and heavy in a velvet blue sky. Lying there he had suddenly heard a voice calling him from on high.

Despite the excitement of living in Terah's house which was always filled with people coming and going, with intrigue, with bickering, and, despite the feverish bustling activities one found on the streets of Ur, Avrom had not been happy there. From early childhood he sensed that he was living in an alien land. He had always seemed different and a stranger. "Aramean dog," they had called him on the streets of Ur as they chased after him with sticks and stones. "You don't belong with us," was the cry. Why could he not have been born a Sumerian like the other children

[2] Robert Graves and Raphael Patai, *Hebrew Myths: The Book of Genesis* (Garden City: Doubleday and Co., 1964), 135.

around him? He had wondered even as a child if he were always going to be different. He chuckled again—now he was truly different.

The sky above him seemed to be getting bluer, and the sand under his feet seemed to be taking on a more purplish hue. The silence around him seemed to take on an air of expectancy and the hills in the distance, much closer now, appeared breathlessly eager as though they were feeling the rush and sweep of God's unfailing wings.

Avrom had run away from home that earlier afternoon after he had been beaten by Terah, his father the idol-maker, because while taking care of his father's shop of idols he had, in disgust and disbelief, smashed them all into bits. He explained to Terah that the largest idol had quarreled with the others and in his anger had destroyed them. Terah was amazed and shocked. He called Avrom a fool, saying idols could do no such things. Avrom, in turn, disturbed his father more by answering that their gods were only stone images and not real gods at all and worshipping them was false, sacrilegious, and immoral.

That night while lying under a carob tree he heard a voice calling him—a voice coming from a star which looked like a diamond in the center of a crown. Avrom felt as though he were floating on a cloud as he ran home through the night. "I am Yahveh," the voice thundered. "No idol-maker formed me. I am the God of the heavens above and of the earth beneath and of the waters under the earth: there is none else. Lift up thine eyes and look, Avrom, as the day pours forth speech and night after night declares knowledge. Lift up thine eyes on high, Avrom, and see: who created these? He who brings out their host by numbers, calling them all by name; by the greatness of his might, and, because he is strong in power not one is missing. He who made the sun, and the stars, and the lands, and turns deep darkness into morning and darkens the day into night, who calls for the waters of the sea and pours them out upon the surface of the earth, the Lord is his name. Despair not, Avrom, Yahveh hears and answers prayers. Forget not, that I, the Lord, have a purpose for the life of Terah's youngest son, not for a day, or a year, or even a generation but for the ages."

Now Avrom understood what the wise men had meant when they said: "If you move one single pebble on the beach you set up a new pattern among the stars and everything on earth will be changed to the end of time."

Avrom's memory stirred deeply as he recalled that hour—he was frightened, bewildered, and exalted. At first he could not accept that vision, he could not listen to that voice, he could not believe what he heard; but as time went on he could listen, he could hear, he could accept and believe more and more until, finally, like a bolt of lightning illuminating a dark sky, a flash of perception lighted Avrom's mind, and he lifted his arms to the heavens and prayed: "What am I going to do? What can I believe? Who is going to be my God?" And the answer came clear: "So live that many may hear me through you and thus follow after the one true God." And Avrom answered: "Oh most high God, give me the strength, the knowledge, the faith to fulfill the plan you have made for me and the thousand generations which will follow me."

The golden emptiness of the desert was disappearing as the sun dropped behind the hills, and a pale moon began to rise. The silence and majesty of the rolling waves of white, glistening sand turning purple like a broad ocean stretching far beyond the sight of man; the sad splendor of the setting sun, the landscape becoming more weird as the cool moonlight bathed it in its blue wash—all these things stirred in Avrom a vague yearning for a distant tomorrow, a feeling he could neither grasp nor understand. All he did know was that there was a voice calling him from the hills across the desert wilderness.

For years during his life in Ur he continued to speak to his new God, to question and argue with Him, to plead for His blessing.

"Oh Lord, how can I know thee? Where can I find thee? Thou art as close to me as breathing and yet art farther than the farthermost star. Thou art as mysterious as the vast solitude of the night and yet art as familiar to me as the light of the sun."

"Thou canst not see my face, Avrom, but I will make all my goodness pass before thee."

"Show me thy face, oh God. How shall I know that thou wilt be with me?"

"God is not a man that He should lie. He hath spoken and shall He not fulfill? I am ever more the same, I am the first and the last: my hand laid the foundations of the earth. My right hand spread the skies above; whenever I call them, they answer my summons. Look, Avrom, at the vast, mysterious world that lies before you, the world of seas and skies, of hills and stars, the world of continents and of centuries, the world of peoples and generations yet unborn. I am God alone!"

"Where dwellest then my soul?" asked Avrom. And the answer came back: "Your soul dwells in memories, in hopes, in God."

"Thou art the first and the last, the Lord of all generations. Thou rulest the world in kindness and all thy creatures in mercy. Thou art my guardian and my strength who sleepeth not and slumbereth not."

The evening sky was pale, still hushed like a thing asleep. Avrom stood naked between the blue sky and the purple sand. Time seemed to be running through his hands, and the pounding of his heart seemed to be taking him into a strange and unknown future. Suddenly, in the heavens a million stars came out, and he could hear springs gushing forth in the valleys, flowing between the hills.

"Put away the gods which your father served on the other side of the river . . . and serve me . . . and fear me, for the fear of the Lord is the beginning of wisdom . . . and get thee out of thy country and from thy kindred, and from thy father's house unto the land that I will show thee. And I will make of thee a great nation, and I will bless thee, and in thee shall all the families of the earth be blessed . . . look at the stars of heaven and try to count them, for your posterity shall be no less numerous. . . . And I will make thy name great and be thou a blessing. . . . Tell your people, Avrom, that they shall become holy, for I am holy."

"I pray thee, Oh Lord, give me a sign to take on my way and to show them."

"I will give thee for a covenant of the people, for a light among the nations, to open the blind eyes, to bring out the prisoners from prison, and them that sit in darkness in the prison house. Go, Avrom, follow the voice that crieth in the wilderness and follow the righteousness of God. I know the future and I know the past. I will remember my covenant forever, the word I command thee and the thousand generations to come after thee. Arise and shine, Avrom, for thy light has come and the glory of the Lord is risen upon thee. Go hence unto the land I will show thee."

"*Vayelekh Avrom*," and "Avrom went."

"I hear your voice, Oh Lord, and I stand before thee in the inescapable light of thy truth, stripped of all pretense. Look with compassion on me as with deep humility I stand before thee. Let the words of my mouth and the meditations of my heart be acceptable in thy sight, my Rock and my Redeemer. I hear your voice, Almighty, and it reminds me of the sound of a ram's horn echoing and re-echoing among the hills."

"And it shall come to pass, Avrom, in that day that a great horn shall be blown throughout the land—the long tone of the ram's horn and in generations to come my voice will be renewed as your followers hear the call of the *Shofar*, so all of you who live on this earth, when the Shofar is heard, listen well, and when the great trumpet is blown come all of you, and worship the Lord—who will be a shield unto you. I command you, listen well to the haunting call of the ram's horn, 'Tekia G'dolah (Awaken ye sleepers).' "

The blue quiet of night had come when peace begins to brood on the desert sand. Nearby Avrom could see the hills, and above the din of the ever-blowing desert wind Yahveh's voice was heard saying: "These words which I command you this day shall be upon thy heart . . . and thou shalt talk of them when thou sittest in thy house, and when thou walkest by the way and when thou liest down and when thou risest up. I am the Lord thy God."

In Avrom's heart there burned a flame; in all the prophets and teachers who would follow him there would be such a flame.

Avrom lay down on his pillow in peace and in sleep: "I will say of the Lord, He is my refuge and my fortress. My God, in Him will I trust. He shall be a lamp unto my feet and a light unto my path. It shall all come to pass in the end of days. . . ."

In his sleep Avrom sighed deeply and reached out a hand as if to grasp the infinite.

III

Honor Thy Father and Thy Mother

And the Lord said: "Thou shalt love the Lord thy God with all thy heart, with all thy soul, and with all thy might. And these words which I command thee this day shall be upon thy heart. Thou shalt teach them diligently unto thy children and shalt speak of them when thou sittest in thy house, when thou walkest by the way, when thou liest down and when thou risest up. Thou shalt bind them for a sign upon thy hand and they shall be frontlets between thine eyes. Thou shalt write them upon the doorposts of thy house and upon thy gates: that ye may remember and do all my commandments and be holy unto thy God." And the Jews answered: *"Na'aseh Ve'nishma"*— "We will do and be obedient" (Exod. 24:7).

It is interesting to note that the allusions to the "sign upon thy hand," "frontlets between thine eyes," and "the doorposts of thy house," refer to *Tefillim* and the *Mezuzah*. *Tefillim* (prayer) applies to the two black leather cubes provided with long leather straps which were worn in biblical days and are worn today by the ultra-Orthodox Jews (over the age of thirteen) during the daily morning prayers (except on the Sabbath and on holidays). The cases contain prescribed passages from the Torah written on strips of parchment and relate to the injunctions concerning Tefillim. One Tefillim tube, called *Shel Yad*, is placed on the left arm facing the heart, and the

other cube, called *Shel Rosh*, is placed in the center of the forehead.
The long leather thong of the Shel Rosh is looped to permit the adjustment of the cube to the skull.

The wearing of Tefillim is in conformity with a biblical commandment and is a reminder that the Torah must be studied and obeyed
every day. The Mezuzah is a small metal or wooden case containing
a strip of parchment on which are inscribed the first two sections of
the liturgical Shema (i.e. Shema and *Vehayah Nu Shamoa*, Deuteronomy 6:4–9 and 11:13–21, each of which prescribes this commandment). The scriptural verse in the Mezuzah speaks of the Jew's
obligation to love God, and obey His commandments. The reverse
side of this parchment bears the name *Shaddai* (Almighty). This case
is attached on the right (as one enters) doorpost of the house. The
word "Mezuzah" literally means doorpost.

Indeed, the Jewish temple was a house of prayer as well as a house
of study—the *Bet ha-Keneset* and the *Bet ha-Midrash*—and the
Jewish home was an organized system of life based on the Torah (and
later on the Talmud) which embodied the great ideals of their prophets, poets, and sages. The family thus became a sort of theocracy, a
group of people devoted to the single-God ideal. Knowledge of Yahveh was their idea of wisdom, worshipping Him was their idea of
virtue, and serving their neighbor was their idea of justice. The important business in their lives was to observe the laws handed down
by their God, to keep the rules of piety expressed in these laws, always conscious that their dead were living all around them, watching
with eager anticipation how their descendants would deal with the legacy they left them when they passed on. The remarkable thing is
that those primitive Hebrews somehow grasped the basic sociopsychological principle that the most vital and equally fundamental thing
to do with their legacy was to pass it on to their own children generation after generation and that the ideal place in which to do this
was the family. Where else and under what other circumstances could
one achieve the idea which has been uppermost with Jews—the idea
of obedience and conduct, conduct and obedience? For it is written

in Proverbs (22:6): "Train up a child in the way he should go: and when he is old he will not depart from it." There is, indeed, a strange paradox in the human being—he is created and yet he creates, he is a product, yet he produces, he belongs in the world, yet he is above it.

Long, long before Thoreau spoke these wise words, the ancient Jews recognized that "for an impenetrable shield stand inside yourself." They discovered that those who can do this will never feel hopelessly insecure. This quality is something not inherited but which one must build for himself painfully and laboriously. It is difficult and costly, achieved often at the expense of "external" security. Here, then, is the heart of the formula which constitutes the socialization process of the individual Jew, the process whereby he was and is made an integral part of his group. History demonstrates that it has been a highly successful formula.

It is well known that the chief source of the Judaic way of life is the Bible. Rabbi Bernard Bamberger brings to us a most unusual awareness of the many aspects of this wellspring of human development in his words: "The chief value of the Bible is not its literary power, its pervasive influence on Western Culture, or its usefulness for Jewish self-comprehension. [But rather in] its profound insight into human behavior, its unfailing concern for human needs, its exacting morality, its insistence on a righteous social order, its vision of the reconciliation of mankind in brotherhood and peace, its tremendous intuitions about man, the world and God, its sublime poems of worship and inspiration—all these speak to us with a force we cannot disregard."[1] As a matter of fact, it is in the fourth Book of Maccabees where there is summed up in one sentence the essential teachings of the Bible, the basic philosophy of Judaism as well as of the philosophy most people in the world seem to be trying to live by. "For in the day when God created man, He implanted in him his passions and inclinations, and also at the very same time, set the mind on a throne amid the senses to be his sacred guide in all things; and

---

[1] Bernard J. Bamberger, *The Bible: A Modern Jewish Approach* (New York: Schocken Books, 1963), 84.

to the mind He gave the Law, by which if a man order himself, he shall reign over a kingdom, that is temperate and just and virtuous and brave."

Oddly enough, those ancients recognized the fact that this ideal, this philosophy, this guide for living would not survive just because it was sound and noble. They understood it would survive and be useful only if it were brought down into the hurly-burly of every-day life, and it was the family circle which must bring it down and ultimately become the school for mankind, the place where the child that was begins to study the rules by which he may become a well-adjusted member of the realm of human beings in general, and, in the case of the Jews, a reflection of the image of that particular group. This concept of reflecting the "image" is a very serious matter in the life of every Jew, for the entire structure of the Hebraic code of ethics and Israel's deep concern over human dignity may be said to rest upon the doctrine implied in the following ideal: "And God created man in His own image, in the image of God created He him; . . ." (Gen. 1:27). It may be said, then, that man's uniqueness lies in the fact that, albeit he is made of physical matter like all other creatures, he alone is allied to God by his very nature. Martin Buber has an exciting observation to make regarding the concept of the "image." He says: "Man is not the image of God, but he is created in the image of God, and if the image is wiped out, man no longer exists as man."[2]

The examination of a wide range of material, including historical events, cultural elements, such as artifacts, sociofacts, and mentifacts, expressions of religious principles, codes of ethics, and goals indicates that biblical Jews had already developed a surprisingly sound and wholesome concept of home and family life. They realized that in order to achieve maximum flexibility in behavior—imperative to survival—the child needs the conditioning of those immediately around him. From this fact alone stems one of the most profound and far-reaching sociological implications—the need and importance of the primary group situation. In short, the beginning of life is far more

---

[2] Buber, *Israel and the World*, 212.

important in the matter of development than any other time in the life cycle.

It has been wisely said that the best index to the degree of advancement achieved by any social group is its treatment of children, women, and the aged. If this be true then the culture of the biblical Jews reached a remarkably high degree of refinement.

Among Jews, children were always looked upon as God's blessing. There are a number of scriptural verses to support this belief. "Lo, children are a heritage of the Lord: . . ." (Psalms 127:3), and further, "Thy children [will be] like olive plants round about thy table" (Psalms 128:3). Equally important in this regard is the contention on the part of Jews that the Torah was given by God not because of Moses, or the priests, or sages, or people in general, but because of the children. It was another of those bargains the Jews made with God. For the Torah they pledged their children to God.

Of the wife and mother it is written: "Who can find a virtuous woman? For her price is far above rubies. The heart of her husband doth safely trust in her, so that he shall have no need of spoil" (Proverbs 31:10–11). Finally, it is written in the Talmud: "Be careful not to cause woman to weep, for God counts her tears. Israel was redeemed from Egypt on account of the virtues of its women. He who weds a good woman, it is as if he fulfilled all the precepts of the law. It is woman alone through whom God's blessings are vouchsafed to a house."

The aged were especially honored in biblical days. Jews have ever vehemently boasted of the glories of their forefathers, sages, prophets, and teachers. To this day one finds in the prayer book for Jewish worship the statement: "Praised be thou, O Lord, God of our fathers, God of Abraham, Isaac and Jacob." Ecclesiastes, who in Hebrew is known as "Ben-Sira," and whose writings are included in the Apocrypha, has this to say regarding Our Fathers:

> Let us now praise famous men
> Our fathers in their generations.
> The Lord manifested in them great glory,
> Even His mighty power from the beginning.

Their bodies are buried in peace
And their name liveth for evermore.
People will declare their wisdom
And the congregation telleth out their praise.

Thus is has been that throughout their history Jews have put their
faith in and fortified their minds with the songs of Solomon, the poetry
of David, the vision of Moses, and the dreams of Avrom.

Finally, in regard to parenthood in general, it is written: "Children's children are the crown of old men; and the glory of children
are their fathers" (Proverbs 17:6). And of the home Rabbi Yose
Ben Joezer has said: "Let thy house be a meeting place for the sages
and sit in the very dust of their feet, and thirstily drink in their
words."

Thus it was that those early Hebrews hit upon an ideal of family
life that was unique then and is still unique among many people. They
conceived the idea that a family unit is not merely a group where
parents and children came together to eat, sleep, work, and interact;
rather it is a "place" where miraculous things happen which result
in security and wisdom, where people grow and mature, and find
strength and inspiration to face the world. They sensed furthermore
that if these things happen it is only because the members of the
family all give of themselves to make them happen. The Jewish
family in those days, as well as throughout most of its history, was a
living illustration of the profound truth that life's every meaning may
be found in the investment one makes of his own best energies, af-
fections, patience, inspirations, and in the personal sacrifices he must
make for the values and goals he deeply believes in.

Israel Abrahams, in his dynamic analysis, *Jewish Life in the Middle
Ages*, observes that "the Synagogue was the center of (Jewish) life
but it was not the custodian of thought."[3]   Indeed, it is the family
which has been the custodian of Jewish thought throughout the ages.
Even in those far-off times and faraway places Jews realized that,
albeit all men must ultimately go along the same pathway, Jews, in

[3] Israel Abrahams, *Jewish Life of the Middle Ages* (New York: Meridian
Books, 1961), xvii.

the light of their particular history, unique experiences, and splendid legacy, must go with a special urgency and with an exceptional devotion, and that it was the family which was the fountainhead of these characteristics. The family thus constituted the nucleus of Hebrew social life, and the bond existing between members of a family was the strongest cement in their social order. One of its major sources of vitality was tradition, the collective memory of their past history during which time family members were forced to unite, to work together, to follow their religious rituals, and to act as a group in order to survive. The strong family sense of such prominent individuals as Avrom, Isaac, Jacob, and Moses was nourished by memories of the roles these families had played in the Jewish saga.

Of the 613 precepts which every Jew was commanded to obey, that concerning reproduction was considered one of the most important, for the very first *Mitzvah* (commandment) in the Torah is "Be fruitful, and multiply, and replenish the earth" (Gen. 1:28). In Jewish tradition this is interpreted as an obligation on every Jewish couple to have a minimum of two children. Folklore has it that Yahveh, to prepare for this eventuality, in His infinite wisdom created during the first six days of creation all the souls of all the human beings who were ever born or ever will be born. These souls reside in the Garden of Eden and were present at the time God made His covenant with the children of Israel. This belief was based on the statement made by Moses in Deuteronomy 29:14–15: "Neither with you only do I make this covenant and this oath; but with him that standeth here with us this day before the Lord our God, and also with him that is not here. . . ." Hebraic tradition also has it that the Messiah could not come until all the souls created by God had been fitted to the earthly bodies for their reception on earth.

The legend further tells us that at the very moment when a child is conceived God asks one of His special angels to look after its proper development.[4] The angel brings the infant before God Himself who then and there decides upon its future destiny: whether it

<hr>

[4] W. M. Feldman, The *Jewish Child* (London: Bailliere, Tindall and Cox, 1917), 146.

will be a male or female, strong or weak, rich or poor, tall or short, attractive or ugly. According to the legend-makers, not even God would assume responsibility for the future behavior of the child. He left that up to the child's subsequent "free will." God then asks that angel whose job it is to look after souls to place the appropriate soul within the infant and return it to its mother's womb. There are times, of course, when the "soul-keeper" either by accident or by design fails to give even one soul to an individual or perhaps gives two souls to another one. The one without a soul ends up being a failure in life, whereas the one with the extra soul becomes outstanding. This explains that intangible quality in great men: it is simply a matter of having *neshoma yethera* (added soul).

Furthermore it is significant to note that when God created souls He created them in pairs, male and female. Afterward, if they deserve it, the complementary pairs are united in marriage and the union is a happy one, otherwise the souls are mismatched and the union is a failure.

A theological view of the Judaic marriage and family life must begin with many affirmations which relate these institutions to Yahveh's purposes. The creation story in Genesis indicates a profound theological treatment of Yahveh's concern about and the ordering of human existence. Genesis 1:26, 27 affirms the creation of man as male and female. "And God said, 'Let us make man in our image, after our likeness;' . . . So God created man in His own image, in the image of God created He him; . . . And God blessed them, . . ." Thus male and female coexistence reflects the image of God. In the *Mishna* there may be found a most thought-provoking anecdote regarding the creation of Adam. "Adam was created single to teach us that to destroy one person is to destroy a whole world, and to preserve one person is to preserve a whole world; that no man shall say to another: 'My father was superior to yours' . . . that though no two men are exactly alike, God stamped us all with the same mold, the seal of Adam; that no one must say: 'The world was created for my sake.'"

Genesis 2:18–23 affirms the ordinance of marriage as God's remedy for human loneliness. "The Lord God said, 'It is not good that the man should be alone; I will make him a helpmate.' . . . And the Lord God caused a deep sleep to fall upon Adam, and he slept; and he took one of his ribs, and closed up the flesh instead thereof; and the rib, which the Lord God had taken from man, made he a woman, and brought her unto the man. And Adam said, 'This is now bone of my bones and flesh of my flesh: she shall be called Woman, because she was taken out of man.' " This passage portrays the man choosing the woman as the one being among all creatures who is particularly qualified for the life partnership with him and who can best help him fulfill the purposes God intended for mankind.

The passionate concern with the family among the Hebrews is indicated by the fact that of the Ten Commandments—called by the Jews the ten words—two are related to the family.

The fifth commandment, "Honor thy father and thy mother: that thy days may be long upon the land which the Lord thy God giveth thee" (Exod. 20:12), sanctifies the family as second only to the Temple in the structure and function of Jewish society. The ideals and patterns stamped upon it in biblical times have characterized it through medieval ages, through the shtetl period, and even to some degree in twentieth-century America. The ancient Hebrew patriarchal family was a closely knit institution composed of the eldest married male, his wife or perhaps wives, his married sons with their wives and children, and in many cases some slaves. This organization was valuable for its economic contribution to society—cultivating the soil, raising sheep and goats, preparing food, clothing and shelter. Its political value lay in its capacity to bring about order and group solidarity.[5]

The government of the biblical Jews was based not on the principles of the state but rather on the patriarchal family structure. The eldest head of each family group participated in a council of elders which was the final court of law and justice in the tribe. The close-

---

[5] Will Durant, *Our Oriental Heritage* (New York: Simon and Schuster, 1954), 333.

ness of the family, the interdependence of its members economically, socially, and spiritually, constituted the sources of its strength, its loyalty, its powers, its goals, and its authority which ramified itself in many directions. This sort of family makeup, with its emotional quality and particular motivation, actually helped to soften the rigors of patriarchal discipline and create the ideals which the prophets recalled in later generations.

This was indeed an excellent example of the patriarchal family. The father's authority was practically unlimited. All property was his; the children belonged to him and he "ruled" his wife. (Thy desire shall be to thy husband and he shall rule over thee.) Incidentally, the Hebrew word for wife is *beulah* which means "owned." Small wonder Lilith would have none of it!

Yet in practice it would seem that family life was actually somewhat democratic, for the very molding force which was responsible for all the stringent laws, customs, and traditions pertaining to marriage and family life, and which directed the lifelong conduct of its members, contains elements which appear to be "civilized" beyond the times. For example, here we find a group of primitive people whose folk life exalted motherhood; who believed that "no blessing enters the home save through the wife; who admonished their children, "Ye shall fear every man his mother, and his father, . . ." (Lev. 19:3); who permitted women to hold positions of high authority and dignity;"[6] who believed that "Unless the Lord build the house, they labor in vain who build it"; and finally who included in their ten basic laws of life the commandment, "Thou shalt not commit adultery."

The seventh commandment recognizes marriage as the basis of the family as the fifth recognizes the family as the basis of society, and it offers to Jewish marriage and family all the support of the Torah. Albeit the commandment does not mention relationships be-

---

[6] Jewish history is filled with names of such women: Sarah, Rachel, Miriam, and Esther. There was also Deborah who was one of the Judges of Israel. And among the forty-eight prophets of Israel, seven were women: Sarah, Meriam, Deborah, Hannah, Abigail, Huldah, and Esther.

fore marriage, there are other regulations which place the burden of proof of the bride's chastity upon her shoulders.

Because the Hebrew group was small in number, unique in outlook, and always struggling for survival, there was great need to increase and multiply, therefore, it exalted motherhood, branded celibacy as a sin, made marriage compulsory after twenty, even for priests, abhorred childless women,[7] and looked upon any form of limiting population as an abomination. Marriage was viewed by the early Jews with great reverence, and a wife was considered a joy to her husband. Indeed, the very name for marriage in Hebrew, *Kiddushim*, means the "ceremony of sanctification." One recalls that Isaac's marriage to Rebekah comforted him for his mother's death (Gen. 24:67). It is evident from the teachings and symbolism of the prophets that marriage, as the ancient Jews understood it, was of divine origin and possessed a divine character. The prophets often picture God as the husband and Israel as the wife. The covenant between husband and wife was so sacred that they could conceive of this as binding God and Israel together.[8] Marriage, therefore, according to the teaching of Judaism is a consecration and a sanctification of life. Its purpose was and is to hallow and sanctify the relationship of husband and wife, as it is the purpose of every commandment to hallow and sanctify conduct. This concept of marriage is expressed in those ancient words the bridegroom utters during the wedding ceremony and the bride also repeats: *"Hare at mekudeshet li"*—"Be thou consecrated unto me."[9]

One is inclined to believe that romantic love played a very minor role among the early Hebrews in the choice of mates. Marriages were usually arranged by parents. Instances of captive marriage are found in the Bible. Yahveh actually approved of it in times of war. "When thou goest forth to war against thine enemies and the Lord

[7] Rachel, when she had no children, said to Jacob: "Give me children or else I die" (Gen. 30:1), and when she had her first child, she said: "God has gathered in my shame" (Gen. 30:2–3).

[8] S. E. Goldstein, *Meaning of Marriage and Foundations of the Family: A Jewish Interpretation* (New York: Bloch Publishing Co., 1942), 13.

[9] *Ibid.*, 12.

thy God hath delivered them into thine hands and thou hast taken
them captive, and seest among the captives a beautiful woman and
hast a desire unto her, that thou wouldst have her to thy wife; then
thou shalt bring her home to thine house; . . . [she should not be
treated as a slave]" (Deut. 21:10–14).

In some cases (Judges 21:20, 21) stealing wives was suggested.
"Go and lie in wait in the vineyards; and see, and, behold, if the
daughters of Shiloh come out to dance in dances, then come ye out
of the vineyards, and catch you every man his wife of the daughters
of Shiloh, and go to the land of Benjamin." Usually the marriage
was by purchase—Jacob obtained Leah and Rachel by working for
their father for fourteen years (Gen. 31:15). Ruth was simply bought
by Boaz (Ruth 4:10). There is at least one case in the Bible where
a man won his wife by his valor. King Saul promised his daughter
to the man who could kill Goliath (I Sam. 17:25). David finally
married Michal, Saul's daughter (18:27) who, incidentally, helped
save David's life when her father planned to kill him (19:11).

Despite this apparent encouragement to go out and get wives
endogamy was actually the rule. "Let them marry to whom they
think best; only to the family of the tribe of their father shall they
marry. So shall not the inheritance of the children of Israel remove
from tribe to tribe: . . ." (Num. 36:6, 7). Intermarriage with those
of other faiths was prohibited for many reasons, the most important
having to do with the survival of the group. "Neither shalt thou make
marriages with them; thy daughter thou shalt not give unto his son,
nor his daughter shalt thou take unto thy son. For they will turn
away thy son from following me, that they may serve other gods: . . ."
(Deut. 7:3, 4). One may recall the bitterness with which Ezra attacked the problem in Palestine when the Jews returned from Persia
with their foreign wives. "And when I heard this thing, I rent my
garment and mantle, and plucked off the hair of my head and of my
beard and sat down astonished" (Ezra 9:3). He went so far as to
induce the community leaders to dissolve such marriages (Ezra
10:3). "Now therefore let us make a covenant with our God to put
away all the wives, and such as are born of them, according to the

counsel of my Lord, . . ." As a matter of fact, the entire question of interfaith marriage has caused much disturbance in Jewish life. The Jews learned early that interfaith marriage, as a rule, meant the loss of Jewish men and women to other groups. Even if the non-Jew of a mixed marriage became a member of the Jewish faith an alien element was introduced which might easily prove to be a source of weakness and danger. The Jews discovered long ago that the culture of a people cannot be maintained intact if foreign and antagonistic elements are allowed to enter it.

Because of this attitude the Jews were probably the "purest" of all groups of the Near East, for they intermarried only very reluctantly with other people. Hence they have maintained their type with astonishing tenacity. The historian Will Durant has a colorful observation to make regarding this phenomenon. "The Hebrew prisoners on the Egyptian and Assyrian reliefs, despite the prejudice of the artist, are recognizably like the Jews of our time. There too, are the long and curved Hittite nose, the projecting cheek bones, the curly hair and beard; though one cannot see under the Egyptian caricature, the scrawny toughness of body, the subtlety and obstinacy of the spirit that have characterized the Semites from the stiff-necked followers of Moses to many of them in modern life."[10]

Oddly enough, despite their deep fear of interfaith marriage and their adamant stand against it, there existed also this wholesome paradoxical attitude—that children born to a Jew whose spouse is Gentile but who is charitable, honest, sincere, gentle, and kind-hearted, must be preferred to children of a Jewish partner who lacks these qualities. The Talmud explains why. "Marry the daughter of a man of character, for as a tree so are its fruit," and also "a good and virtuous wife expands a man's character."

The Bible and later the Talmud sanctioned polygamy but tradition favored monogamy. Moses had at least two wives. Isaac had

---

[10] Durant, *Our Oriental Heritage*, 302–03. Speaking of the Hittite nose, it should be noted that the mingling of Jews with non-Jews in Western Europe and in America is beginning to give them a sharply aquiline nose, so that this particular characteristic may now be considered "Aryan."

but one wife, and his son Jacob really wanted only one, but was tricked into marrying two, and Solomon—there is no point in even mentioning his outlook on polygamy. Avrom had one wife until it became evident that she could not bear him a child. It was then that Sarah convinced him to take a second wife, Hagar, who did bear him a son, Ishmael. Later when Sarah finally gave birth to Isaac she became jealous of Hagar and her child and drove them both out into the desert. Sarah never dreamed that the proverbial typically feminine prerogative of changing her mind would, four thousand years later, result in a serious and tragic problem affecting Jewry in particular and the world in general; that, in the twentieth century, the followers of the half-brothers in Avrom's tent would be facing each other across the River Jordan with hatred in their heart and guns in their hands. For the Lord even then vaguely cautioned Avrom about his two sons, ". . . in Isaac shall seed be created to thee. And also of the son of the bondwoman I will make a nation because he is thy seed" (Gen. 17:19). And, furthermore, God even warned Hagar about her child: "His (Ishmael's) hand will be against every man, and every man's hand against him; . . ." (Gen. 16:12). Indeed, it has all come to pass, for the Israelis are the offspring of Isaac and the Arabs are the offspring of Ishmael.

It is true that in Jewish law it is the husband who marries and not the court, and it is the husband who divorces and not the court. Divorce was free to the man but extremely difficult for the woman (Deut. 24:1). There were, however, two conditions which could prohibit a man from getting a divorce: if he falsely accused his wife of immorality, and if he attacked a girl. In the latter instance he must marry her, "because he hath humbled her, he may not put her away all his days" (Deut. 22:29). As has been noted, traditionally it was the husband who could break the marriage; however, if the wife had valid reasons she might divorce her husband. Among the cases warranting such action the Talmud lists the following: the husband's impotence, failure of support, denial of conjugal rights, contraction of a loathsome disease, or working at a repugnant occupation. The divorced woman was protected by the *Ketubah* (marriage contract), which provided a financial settlement for her and her children's care.[11]

Throughout the centuries the teachers of Judaism have actually disapproved of divorce and by various enactments have discouraged it. "Let none deal treacherously against the wife of his youth. For the Lord, . . hateth putting away: . . ." (Malachi 2:15, 16). The Talmud regards divorce as the greatest of all family tragedies. "Who so ever divorces the wife of his youth even the Altar sheds tears on her behalf. As it is written 'and this again ye do, ye come to the Altar of the Lord with tears . . . because the Lord hath been witness between thee and the wife of thy youth against whom thou has dealt treacherously.' " Throughout the Talmud it is emphasized again and again that no sacrifice is too great to effect the reconciliation of husband and wife. However, when husband and wife simply cannot live together in harmony, the Talmud sanctions divorce as preferable to a life of bitterness and strife.

The founding of a family was regarded in biblical Judaism not merely as a social ideal but as a religious duty. Furthermore, the early Jews invested marriage with the highest communal significance. Only he who founded a house in Israel was worthy to be considered a full-fledged member of the community; only she who had become a mother in Israel had realized her destiny.

The last chapter of Proverbs presents a picture of the ideal wife and mother and, even though it is slightly biased on the side of the male, it offers an attitude which has persisted throughout Jewish history and has profoundly influenced Jewish family life wherever it existed:

> Who can find a virtuous woman?
> For her price is far above rubies.
> The heart of her husband doth safely trust in her,
> So that he shall have no need of spoil.
> She doeth him good and not evil
> All the days of her life.

[11] Ben Zim Bokser, *Wisdom of the Talmud* (New York: The Citadel Press, 1962), 112.

She seeketh wool and flax,
And worketh willingly with her hands.

.   .   .   .

She girdeth her loins with strength,
And maketh strong her arms.

.   .   .   .

She stretcheth out her hand to the poor;
Yea, she reacheth forth her hands to the needy.

.   .   .   .

Her husband is known in the gates,
When he sitteth among the elders of the land.

.   .   .   .

Strength and dignity are her clothing;
And she shall rejoice in time to come.
She openeth her mouth with wisdom;
And in her tongue is the law of kindness.

.   .   .   .

Her children rise up, and call her blessed;
Her husband also and he praiseth her:
Many daughters have done virtuously,
But thou excellest them all.
Grace is deceitful, and beauty is vain;
But a woman that feareth the Lord,
She shall be praised.
Give her of the fruit of her hands;
And let her works praise her in the gates.

Jewish tradition stressed chastity of both man and woman before marriage, matrimonial fidelity on both sides, desire for large families, respect of children for their parents, and unlimited love and devotion of parents for their children. To this day, Jews read in their prayer books during the Friday evening services this very significant passage: "At this hour, O God, thy messenger of peace descends from on high to turn the hearts of the children to the parents, and the hearts of the parents to the children, strengthening the bond of devotion in the home and making it a sanctuary worthy of Thy presence."

Then there is that poem in the Talmud which sums up most beautifully the relationship between children and parents:

> God, your father and your mother
> They have each a share in you.
> If you pay to both your parents
> That respect which is their due,
> Then together with your parents
> God considers He doth dwell;
> And by honoring your parents
> You do honor God as well.

Jewish law states that both the husband and wife have mutual rights but particularly does it protect the wife's essential freedom. According to the Bible, one can believe that sex is not something one has but something one is and, furthermore, the biblical news joyfully affirms that man is a sexual creature and that this is a good thing. This attitude is demonstrated, for instance, in its special concern with the wife's biological peculiarities, her need to be alone as well as her need to be with her husband. Deuteronomy (24:5) makes it clear furthermore, that "when a man hath taken a new wife, he shall not go out to war, neither shall he be charged with any business: but he shall be free at home one year, and shall cheer up his wife . . . ," for "at thy right hand doth stand the queen," says the wedding ode in Psalms (45:9).

Jewish laws regarding the welfare of widows and orphans, the treatment of strangers, as well as the protection of expectant mothers, are well known (Deut. 10:18, 19). "He doth execute justice for the fatherless and widow, and loveth the stranger in giving him food and raiment. Love ye therefore the stranger, for ye were strangers in the land of Egypt."

The authority for the ancient Jewish custom known as levirate—from the Hebrew word meaning "brother-in-law"—obliging the brother of a man who died leaving a widow (but no children) to marry the widow is the twenty-fifth chapter and fifth verse of Deuteronomy. However, in practice this procedure was seldom followed unless the couple was interested in each other and believed they could be happy together.

Orphans were considered as helpless beings. God Himself was

considered the father of the fatherless. He who oppresses orphans is to expect the severest punishment (Exod. 22:21–23). "Thou shall not afflict any widow, or fatherless child. If thou afflict them in any wise, and they cry at all unto me, I will surely hear their cry; and my wrath shall wax hot, and I will kill you with the sword; and your wives shall be widows, and your children fatherless."

Expectant mothers were particularly protected (Ex. 21:22–25). "If men strive and hurt a woman with child, so that her fruit depart from her, and yet no harm follow: he shall be surely punished according as the woman's husband shall lay upon him; and he shall pay as the judges determine. But if any mischief follows then thou shalt give life for a life, eye for eye, tooth for tooth, hand for hand, foot for foot, burning for burning, wound for wound, strife for strife."

In biblical times Jewish women were not to enter public life but were to devote themselves to domestic duties and assist their husbands in their work. As a matter of fact, they exerted tremendous influence within their own sphere of activities. An age-old division of labor kept both sexes happily occupied; each was convinced that both husband and wife were making a real and worthwhile contribution to the family well-being.

The husband's authority over his wife and children rested upon tradition rather than force. Despite the high status of the husband, the wife enjoyed a high position in the Jewish family. She participated in religious festivities and ceremonies. She could possess property and dispose of it, and she could retain her own wealth. Although she could not easily divorce her husband, interestingly enough, she could desert him (Judges 19). So important was motherhood to the wife in early Judaism that the wife, if she were barren and had sufficient authority in the family, could actually demand that her husband take another wife or employ another woman to provide her a vicarious motherhood.

The ancient Hebrews were quite concerned about sterility in women and devised a most ingenious technique to cure it. The woman could plead before God saying: "Lord, if Thou dost not answer my prayers for a child, I shall make my husband suspicious of fidelity and he will then take me to the Priest and have me go through the ordeal by water, and surely Thou will not allow the words of Thy Torah to be false for it is written that if a woman be not defiled but clean, then she shall be free and have children." Since it is well known that the Lord helps those who help themselves, the "doctors" of Biblical days suggested remedies for treatment of sterility in women: (1) Mix the ashes of the burned skin of a fox with water and drink it three times a day for three days; (2) Drink water in which has been cooked moss that has grown on the Temple wall; (3) Try praying again.

There was also a remedy for impotence: take three measures of *kurtemi*, pound and boil them and drink them with wine, which in itself was considered an aphrodisiac. If this did not work, garlic and fish were also recommended, as were mandrake plants (Gen. 30:14–17).

And complementing this attitude, it was forbidden to men to use any means to make themselves sterile. However, women were allowed to avail themselves of such remedies in cases where pregnancy would mean danger for the mother or child. The following was recommended as a draught for sterility or *Kos shel Akarin*: Alexandrian gum, alves, and saffron, in equal parts, triturated well together and drunk in wine. Embryotomy was also performed in certain cases of difficult labor.

A woman needing special help in giving birth could get the services of a midwife. In the Bible the midwife is called *Meyaledeth*, or maternity assistant; two are mentioned by name during the time of the Egyptian bondage, Shipra and Puah (Exod. 1:15).

There has long been a belief among Jews that he who leaves children is never considered dead. The intense longing for children, particularly sons, among the early Hebrews is mirrored in the pages of the Talmud.[12] By a play on words the thought is expressed that children (*banim*) are builders (*bonim*); they not only build the

---

[12] Sons are valuable for many reasons but especially because sons say *Kaddish* (sanctification), which is a prayer recited for the dead for eleven months following death and on the anniversary date.

future of the family but likewise the community and ultimately the entire society.

Even in those days when daughters generally had little value, Jews were admonished that "a man should look at the birth of a daughter as a blessing from the Lord," despite the fact that "a daughter is a doubtful boon to her father, and a constant source of worry. When she is very young one has fears she be seduced; when she becomes of age, lest she does not get married; and when married lest she has no children." Daughters usually remained at home until marriage, which often took place at a very young age.

The first-born son was regarded as the most important child. He had more authority than the other children and enjoyed special rights and privileges, among them being the right of primogeniture which conferred on him the right of a double portion of inheritance, even if he were illegitimate. Every Jewish male child was circumcised on the eighth day after his birth, even if the day happened to be the Sabbath. The reason given by the Talmud for fixing the age of the child at eight days and not earlier is that the rite should not be carried out at a time when everybody is merrymaking while the parents are in sorrow on account of the impurity of the mother. The operation was performed by a *Mohel*, or circumciser, and no Gentile was permitted to perform this rite except when there was no one else available.

There were several reasons for this rite. First and foremost, it was a sign of the covenant between Yahveh and the Jews, and, equally important, it was meant to be a mark of distinction between Jews and non-Jews.[13] Also, it had a purely utilitarian object, cleanliness and an aid to reproduction. Finally, it was meant to be a substitute for human sacrifice.

Believing that everything belonged to their God, the ancient peoples felt that in order to keep most of their possessions they had to return some to the deity in order to keep his will. One of the customs was to offer on the altar their first-born animals. Some even

---

[13] Throughout history this rite has been ridiculed by non-Jews who considered Jewish men marked because of it.

sacrificed their first-born children. Yahveh put a stop to this in the incident of Avrom and his son Isaac. Thus it was that the early Jews gave up the idea of human sacrifice; however, they concluded that at least a small part of the male child should be sacrificed to Yahveh, and from this belief evolved the practice of circumcision.[14]

There is a story told in the Talmud which throws some light on the advanced thinking of the early Hebrews concerning the concept of circumcision. Turmus Rufus, a Roman general, once asked Rabbi Akiba why God did not make man just as He wanted him to be. "Why do you Jews go through the ceremony of circumcision?" Rabbi Akiba answered: "Everything that God created was purposely made incomplete in order that human ingenuity may perfect it. Take, for instance, the acorn and the cake that is made from it. Man is born uncircumcised because it is the duty of man to perfect himself."

A matter which has caused much confusion in the minds of both Jews and Gentiles has been the rite of baptism and its place in the lives of biblical Jews. It is well known, of course, that this ritual of immersion does not now exist among Jews; however, in biblical times if a child was born to heathen parents and was going to be converted to Judaism, it required immersion, known as "baptism" from the Greek word *baptizein* (to dip in water). The purpose of this rite was to cleanse, purify, and initiate. If, however, the mother had embraced Judaism during her pregnancy her own immersion at the time constituted baptism for the child.

The whole concept of death plays a vitally important role in the culture of any group. In Judaism, death was and is looked upon from a two-fold point of view. On the one hand, it recognizes the feeling of loss and provides channels for expressing such natural grief through the laws of mourning. Thus, mourning is made easier and psychologically more sound, particularly since prolonged mourning is forbidden. On the other hand, Judaism teaches that death is not the end although it does not attempt to explain the "world to come."

[14] Allan Tarshish, *Not by Power* (New York: Bookman Associates, 1952), 16.

It suggests that man must simply rely on the justice, mercy, and wisdom of God for the final reckoning.

One major factor which is inescapable in the entire *raison d'etre* of the Jewish family is its sense of responsibility for the training of children. There are the talmudic dicta that a father is reprehensible who does not teach his son a craft. It is his responsibility also to help his son find a wife. The Talmud gives a plan of life for a youth: five years of age, Torah; ten years of age, Mishna; thirteen years of age (responsibility) Bar Mitzvah; fifteen years of age, Talmud; eighteen years of age, marriage; and twenty years of age, work.

Next to spiritual values the most dependable resource the Jews have had throughout their history has been education. They discovered long ago that there was no saturation point in learning, and they would have laughed at Bias, the Greek sage, who preached that "truth breeds hatred."

According to the Mosaic law, it is the responsibility of the father to bring up and educate his children and to teach them "the right way wherein they shall go." About Avrom it was said (Gen. 18:19): "He will command his children and his household after him, and they shall keep the ways of the Lord, to do justice and judgment; . . ." That the mother also had to do with her children's moral education especially in their early youth is made clear in Proverbs (1:8): "My son, hear the instruction of thy father, and forsake not the law of thy mother." Of course, the very heart of the ancients' philosophy, which has influenced Jewish life since that day, was spoken by Job (28:18, 19): "The price of wisdom is above rubies. The topaz of Ethiopia shall not equal it, neither shall it be valued with pure gold."

The central theme of biblical education was implied in the phrase "they shall keep the ways of the Lord, to do justice and judgment." It is accepted that education is sociological in that on any level, in any society, its purpose is to prepare individuals to live in the group in such manner that both the individual and the group will survive. The understanding and appreciation of this concept has been the cardinal source of the lasting power among Jews. As their hope wrestled with disillusionment and their confidence struggled with despair, they quickly developed a group preoccupation with the business of survival, the focal points of which were the commandments of God and the family (which was the medium through which God's words were implemented in everyday living). They seem to have stumbled on the basic idea, which psychologists are now expounding, that childhood is the seed time of the mind. Indeed, "train up a child in the way he should go: and when he is old he will not depart from it." Rabbi Elisha Ben Abuyah's elaboration on this concept bears noting: "He that studies as a child, to what may he be likened? To ink written on fresh paper. But he that studies as an old man, to what may he be likened? To ink written on worn paper."

The Jews' textbooks, sources of knowledge, wisdom, and inspiration were all combined in one library, the Torah—the Mosaic code on which all life was established. Rabbi Elezar Ben Azariah grasped the very essence of this phenomenon when he said: "Where there is no Torah there is no right conduct. Where there is no right conduct there is no Torah. Where there is no wisdom there is no piety, where there is no piety there is no wisdom. Where there is no perception there is no knowledge, where there is no knowledge there is no perception, where there is no bread there is no Torah, where there is no Torah there is no bread." The Torah's importance in the history of social institutions and legal conduct cannot be overestimated. It must be considered as one of the most thoroughgoing attempts in the history of man to use religion as a basis of law and order in every detail of life. Marriage and family life, food and health, personal and public behavior were thus made subjects of divine ordinance.

Engraved upon the hearts and minds of every member of the biblical family was the phrase, *El Kelohanu*—"there is none like our God." It was He who said to them: "Hear O Israel, I am the Lord thy God and there is none else and thou shalt love the Lord thy God with all thy heart and with all thy soul and with all thy might, and I give you a good doctrine; forsake it not."

Here, then, is a brief picture of the Jewish biblical family, to which the individual owed his primary obligation, next only to God. To the ancient Hebrews the cosmic process revealed the plan and the purpose, the will and the destiny of mankind; and the family unit, being the end product, the fruit, the harvest, as it were, was the object, care, and love of God Himself. Judaism has ever taught that the relationship between God and man is akin to that between a loving father and his family. Early Jewish sages recognized there was a "bio-sociopsychological" scheme in the area of family life. They recognized that the "one flesh" union is only a portion of this unique relationship for it spells out other specific aspects of life. There is the matter of parenthood and the power structure of the family group; the challenge, duties, authorities, and responsibilities ascribed to each member of the group; the nature of the growing and maturation processes involved in the offspring; the "sociopsychological" interactions of one member to the other; the personal hopes of the individual and suprapersonal hopes for his group; the intense struggle for survival on the part of each person and of the group as a whole; and finally there is the business of defending the ashes of their fathers and the temples of their God. They firmly believed that the family was the stream of heritage, the bridge between yesterday and today, between today and tomorrow.

Here is a vision of a small social group. It is not a vision composed merely of intangibles, beautiful poetry, wise sayings, and stringent commandments. It is one which was based on stark reality, which had meaning and which existed a long time.

Suddenly in the seventieth year of the Christian era the Jewish commonwealth was destroyed by Titus. On the ninth day of the month of Ab the Temple was burned and "Jerusalem was an habitation of strangers; her festival days were turned into mourning" (I Maccabees). "Once more the daughter of Zion sat and wept for the sanctuary that lay in ashes, for her sons that had fallen by the sword and for her daughters carried away into slavery and given over to dishonor. The nation had been vanquished, yet there remained one thing that the fury of legions was powerless to destroy, the invincible Torah of the Jew."[15]

[15] Max L. Margolis and Alexander Marx, *A History of the Jewish People* (Philadelphia: Jewish Publication Society of America, 1927), 204.

The biblical history of the Jews ends chronologically with Nehemiah's prayer: "Remember me, O my God, for good" (Neh. 13:31). Here begins the dispersion of the Jews. A student of Jewish history says: "It could be that this situation saved Judaism from physical expiration and spiritual inbuilding. Palestine united the dispersed members of the nation and gave them a sense of oneness."[16] They were dispersed but not exterminated. Extermination of an entire ethnic group was left to a more modern and so-called civilized nation of central Europe.

Thus God's Torah and the Jewish family, side by side, along with the haunting echo of the Shofar began their dangerous but glorious journey westward into *Galus* (exile), a journey, every stage of which was a revelation of spiritual depth and extraordinary human experience. Along the way some members became Moslems, some became Sephardic (Spanish) Jews, some became Ashkenazi (German) Jews, some became Marranos, some actually became Christians, but the great mass moved forward as if following instructions carried in the genes, ever continuing to "think otherwise," ever saying the Shema and murmuring the twenty-third Psalm, yet ever looking to the Shepherd alone for guidance.

Today, a plane needs but a few hours to cover the distance between Palestine and Eastern Europe. It took the Jews eighteen hundred years to make the journey from Jerusalem to the shtetl.

[16] Elias Bickerman, *Ezra to the Last of the Maccabees* (New York: Shocken Books, 1962), 3.

IV

A Watch in the Night

Bontzye Schweig challenged God and His heavenly host; the Jews in the shtetl of Eastern Europe challenged the world and all mankind.

The shtetl was more a "life space" than a "physical space." This writer recalls vividly, and with a pain he cannot isolate, that to him the shtetl seemed like a lonesome place set against the distant twilight sky and that, at times, its members appeared like shadows moving through a shadowy world. It was a community based on memory. "A common memory has kept us together and enabled us to survive. . . ."[1] and the whole business of living in the shtetl was part and parcel of that memory, yet its *raison d'etre* had to do with a dream of the future. Indeed, life for the shtetl Jews seemed always to be hanging in the balance between the life of today and the life and hope of the future. The privilege of belonging to a kingdom of priests placed a serious and heavy responsibility on their shoulders. They felt deeply the obligation to demonstrate that they were worthy of the part. On the one hand they found themselves seeking the inner meaning, the regulations, the laws of their conduct, and the truth of their existence in the prosaic acts of everyday life, while on the other hand they believed with equal fervor what they said at their

[1] Buber, *Israel and the World*, 146.

Passover service and through every day of the year: "*I'shonah haba-ah birushalayim*"—"Unto the next year in Jerusalem." The idea behind the call on Passover brings to mind the ideal in Judaism for the hope of the future.

Those unsophisticated people learned along the way to the shtetl that people cannot live on logic alone, that without hope of the future not even God's Torah could save them, so they trained themselves, generation after generation, to concern themselves with the future; they prepared themselves for it, they discussed it, they dreamed of it, and they prayed for it. These Jews, for a long time, had been commandos of the soul. They had been willing to take risks and to venture far into new territories of the spirit, and both they and the rest of the world have profited from their gains. They grasped well the concept that it is the future which sets people free, and they understood equally well that what happens in the future is largely determined by what one does today. Indeed, their eighteen-hundred-year odyssey ground into their beings the notion that history teaches almost everything, even the future.

The Jews of the shtetl had a compulsion to go on living, and from what we know about them, survival seemed to them to be worth any sacrifice, any pain, and any price. Their bitterness and pleasure, their moments of knowing heaven as well as hell are rare moments experienced by few individuals in a lifetime. The very tenacity of the shtetl Jews suggests the confidence of those who draw their strength from within. It is impossible to mistake the origin of this outlook. The roots go down to the deep substrata of Avrom and Moses, Job and Isaiah. There was no pagan luxuriance, there were no riots of color, no exciting perfumes in their universe. The volcanic passions pent up in their hearts were based essentially on God's own dictum given in serious, stately, and challenging form—"no doubt, but ye are the people." The Jews of the shtetl felt God even with their finger tips. What they possessed above all else was *emunah* (faith), but the Hebrew word "emunah" means more than just belief; it means firmness, trust, conscientiousness, truthfulness, and strong convictions.

To discuss the nature of the shtetl within a sociological frame of reference seems like a frightful ordeal. The Jewish communal history throughout the millennium of Diaspora life has long been the subject of considerable scholarly attention. The European community of the pre-emancipation era has, for many years, attracted modern investigation because of its extraordinary characteristics. Its remarkable combination of religious and secular authority, its almost "extra-territorial" status and "sovereign" political powers and the overwhelming influence it had over its members have been the source of much historical and sociological analysis.[2] For one who first saw the reflection of the world from within the confines of a shtetl, it is particularly difficult to fit this clustering of people into any of the classical categories of community studies. One is ever reminded of the Yiddish proverb which says: "For example is no proof." What makes this undertaking even more thorny is the fact that, somehow, by staring into the bright rays of the outside world, members of the shtetl themselves become invisible. Like termites they built sites. They blocked up with tradition, fantasy, and myth (created around a memory core which did have hidden in it a kernel of truth) every chink and cranny through which the scorching light of the outside world might enter. They rolled themselves up into little packages in their own security, in their routine, in their ritual, in the 613 commandments, raising a powerful wall against all the bitter winds of hate and biting tides of intolerance. They never asked themselves questions to which there were no answers. There is a strange paradox involved in this phenomenon. As their insight became more sharpened, their horizon of the world became shorter. It is as though the shtetl were the outcome of some inexplicable cosmic accident or some cosmic design, depending upon one's perspective.

Even the most elementary theorist must accept the idea that at least part of the explanation of the uniqueness of that community can be found in a mysterious ingredient of history. The commonest observation on history is that it does not stand still. This must mean that "it" flows. Whatever it is that flows in Jewish history constitutes the

[2] Salo W. Baron, *The Jewish Community* (Philadelphia: Jewish Publication Society of America, 1945), vii.

very foundation of the shtetl. It is the opinion of this writer that this "it," this mysterious ingredient of Jewish history was an "attitude." Here is an example of a community, a fellowship, an association, with the common denominator being neither nationality, language, nor race, but exclusively a state of mind based on religion, creating a group rationale, an *élan vital*, as it were, the transfiguring power of which propelled the Jews on in their unfinished pilgrimage on earth and to their ultimate purpose in the universe. To such a degree was the power of that "it" in Jewish history that there were times when, as an entire group, they were quite prepared to spend themselves utterly for this value which meant more to them than mere physical survival.

Consciously or unconsciously, willingly or unwillingly, the Jews of the shtetl followed the formula implied in the old adage which states that the way to be safe is never to be overly secure; that each person, each group requires the spur of insecurity to force it to survive. It was Charles Spurgeon who once said that many men owe the grandeur of their lives to their tremendous difficulties, and it was John Ruskin who added that "you may either win your peace or buy it. Win it by resistance to evil, buy it by compromise with evil." The shtetl Jews were a classic example of these philosophic dicta. Indeed, Avrom never dreamed what harvests were to be gathered from his sowings, neither in the form of strength, hope, inspiration, and grandeur, nor in the form of pain, tears, blood, and ashes.[3]

There are, of course, those (both Jews and non-Jews) who persist in their belief that Jews were not and are not now an ethnic group; that, in fact, it was not necessary for them to promote a separate culture. They go so far as to assert that the Judaism of the shtetl was a stratagem by which the Jews hoped to capture and manipulate God. They simply cannot understand why Jews complain so much against

[3] There is a poignant story that is most apropos at this point. In the early 1930's a Japanese mission came to Germany to study the Hitler movement. When a member of the mission was asked what he thought about the movement, he answered that it was magnificent and that it would be wonderful if Japan had something like it—the trouble was, however, that Japan could not, because Japan had so few Jews.

their extermination. This is quite understandable—cries of help are often irksome to the preoccupied humanitarian. The Jews of the shtetl might easily have answered these observers by suggesting that they ask the tightrope walker whether he is really doing what he seems or whether he is only pretending. Rabbi Abraham Joshua Heschel, the contemporary Jewish scholar and philosopher, also has an answer for these commentators. "There is a price to be paid by the Jew. He has to be exalted in order to be normal. In order to be a man, he has to be more than a man. To be a people, the Jews have to be more than a people."[4]

The shtetl Jews believed themselves to be heroes acting in a drama created by God as the playwright. They played their heroic roles before a tremendous and very special audience—their ancestors who were watching them all the time, the rest of the Jews scattered throughout the Diaspora, and even more important, before the generations yet to come.[5] In the shtetl there was not an *am ha-åretz* (ignoramus) so unenlightened that he did not know about his past, nor indifferent enough not to realize that in order for Judaism to survive he must pass on the tradition of his forefathers.

To add to the difficult sociological, anthropological, and geographical task of isolating any universals that may underlie the origin, nature, shape, and content of the shtetl is the fact that there were actually two shtetls in one—the visible and the invisible. What the average Gentile saw was a shadow; he could never even get close to the substance of the real community. Thus it is that in the final analysis the story of the shtetl cannot be explained in terms of a slide rule projection or a blueprint construction. In a sense it was rather an example of a group identification, a cultural island, isolated and separated from the cultural forces of social life on the outside; a case,

[4] Abraham Joshua Heschel, *The Earth Is the Lord's* (New York: Henry Schuman, 1950), 64.

[5] There were also others watching them—those outside the shtetl—those with the cold and uncomprehending eyes; those who would overwhelm them with indignities, not imagined but atrociously and unendurably real; those who, when they saw the actors, reacted only to what was to them their already prefabricated images: the Christ-killer, the usurer, the thorn in their sides, the eternal stranger.

par excellence, of a folk passionately sharing institutions and values, but only among themselves. Here was a group, a neighborhood really, whose emphasis was directed toward the realization of a boundless spiritual search by individuals, dreaming, praying, and working for freedom, social justice, and the fatherhood of God. For this effort they needed a special kind of security and guidance which they received from the Torah, the Talmud, and the incorrigible conviction of their mission in the world. They were imbued above all else with the ideal of self-determination—the call first heard by Avrom in the Haran desert, later echoed by Moses at Mt. Sinai, and re-echoed along the way by Isaiah, Jeremiah, Amos, Micah, and Job. Deep in their very souls they felt that the ultimate freedom is the freedom to discipline oneself. This, they believed, would not only empower them to survive but also to succeed. This self-discipline enabled them to demonstrate a most valuable trait shared by people living in a reciprocal relationship, the process of acting closely together and thus generating a new and dynamic force with which to face the agonizing dilemmas that confronted them. Indeed, "how odd of God, to choose the Jews!"

How, then, does one go about exploring the sociopsychological point in space glibly termed the shtetl, a social phenomenon based, in part, on divine mysteries, surrounded by a sense of eternity, filled with inexplicable powers, packed with all the foibles and tragi-comedies of human nature, saturated with kindness, hope, and beauty as well as frustration, misery, and fear, and now all but vanished from the human scene?[6]

The voice of the shtetl spoke with a strange accent, and it has been wisely said that the accent of one's birthplace persists in the mind and heart as much as in speech. Every Jew in that community reflected this accent—in every word he spoke, in every gesture of his hand, turn of his head, and lift of his eyebrow, in his prayers, in his

[6]Mark Zborowski and Elizabeth Herzog, *Life Is with People* (New York: International Universities Press, 1952), 29. The authors employ a delightful technique in giving a picture of traditional life in the shtetl, using a cultural frame of reference.

daily tasks, in his attitude about his family, his world, and his God. If one could but understand the voice of the shtetl one might get a glimpse of the spirit of the life underneath the artificial coloring created over the centuries and spread like a haze over the entire group living within its confines. If this were possible, perhaps one could experience, at least to some degree, the sensation of watching the petty affairs of his neighbors as they went about pursuing their daily lives and facing their individual life crises. He could thus stand apart for a brief moment and observe their ways and consider their interplay in the lives of each other, and he could even touch the stuff out of which their collective life was really made.

The petty affairs of one's neighbor constituted the very heart and soul of the shtetl. Its members would have disagreed with those eminent sociologists and psychologists who call themselves "behaviorists" and imply that thought, feeling, and imagination do not exist, that everything may be conceived in terms of physiology, which ultimately reduces everything to physics and chemistry. They would have considered this point of view naive. How, they would have asked, can physical and chemical elements feel pain and beauty, tragedy and inspiration?

It is the opinion of the author that the best possible way he can deal with this topic is to discuss the way in which the shtetl expressed itself through its inmates: how they projected themselves, how they felt, judged, and mastered their religious, philosophical, and cultural heritage; and how they did the things necessary to live and survive, from birth to death and even beyond death, including rearing of children, taking care of the aged, learning the word of God, dealing with their non-Jewish neighbors, celebrating their holidays, praying in their synagogues and in their homes, crying at their sorrows, and laughing at their stories, mostly about themselves. This undertaking does not even approximate a truly complete picture of life there; however, it does seem logical to believe that a particularly chosen series of topics illustrating significant areas might give form, substance, and cohesion to a people searching for a self-recognition of their worth and honor and to fulfill the promise made, not by them, but by God: "You shall be unto me a kingdom of priests and a holy nation."

The Jews of the shtetl thought of their community as a microcosm designed and governed by the Almighty who created it from original chaos. "For all the earth is mine," saith the Lord. It was a complex whole, but basically it was characterized by order, reason, and purpose. They believed without doubt that every event in the universe flowed from some previous event and that God, the supreme intelligence, if He so desired, could at any moment unfailingly foretell all its future events until the end of time.

Furthermore, they clearly saw God as the stable Will sustaining the universe and all that is therein, from which Will was generated the universality of the moral law and the absolute authority of divine judgment. The next step in their thinking was natural and simple: from this concept came the ideal of the fatherhood of God and the brotherhood of man. And the third step was equally easy: it was their business, as rational beings, not to argue for what is going to be but rather for what ought to be, in the consciousness that it may be a long time in coming. But, having waited so long, they would continue to wait, for it is written: "A thousand years in Thy sight are but a yesterday when it is past, and as a watch in the night." (Psalms 90:4).

In such a universe then, behavior, human or divine, must of necessity be rooted in reason, order, and purpose. Thus, any act was rational, motivated, and directed toward some goal. Whether it be the negotiation of the *shadchun* (matchmaker), the weight of the dowry "yoke," the wailing of a baby, the tedious preparation of the Passover feast, the joys and tragedies of everyday living, any act must have *tachlis!*[7] If a Jew is to do something he must have a tachlis (purpose); life itself, whether as a whole or in its single activities, must have some tachlis. In fact, for the shtetl Jew the imponderable workings of the entire universe must have tachlis.

The Jews of the shtetl thought carefully and systematically, with

[7] No term was more familiar to the ears of the shtetl Jew than *tachlis*, which means purpose, aim, or goal.

initiative and premeditation. Their action must be concrete and precise; there must be no vagueness, a luxury they could ill afford. They examined with curiosity and urgency their source of life, from which they drew their strength and vitality, their hopes and dreams of the future. They learned quickly, too, that the downtrodden, the underdog, the persecuted must always believe in himself, in his credo, in his purpose, if he is to survive. They learned from their forefathers long before the advent of Patrick Henry that life is never "so dear or peace so sweet as to be purchased at the price of chains and slavery." And, finally, they learned early in life that they had better listen to the voice of the shtetl, for it was more than the voice of the rabbinate, the voice of the leadership, or the voice of the congregation. The voice said that certain things are important, and those are the things for which individual Jews must strive. Their history reminded them quickly and painfully of the consequences when this voice had not been heard in the past. It must be heeded and well, or it may come only in the presence of ignominious death as it did to the thousands who would some day walk in the *schrecklichkeit* (horror) of the streets in Germany. This voice emphasized many things, among them being that there are certain elements in Judaism only which can meet the needs of the human spirit if people are to be part of the group known as Jews.

Indeed, the Jew of Rechicha knew the Jews better than his religious counterpart, the *Berliner Kulturmensch* (a cultured, refined person from Berlin). He could have told him that it is much more difficult to suffer when one does not have an ideal worth suffering for. This was another lesson the Jews had learned well. Like scientists in their laboratories, they made dramatic albeit tragic discoveries which served to demonstrate what otherwise might have remained mere theory and speculation. Personal experiences were far from being their sole authority for their beliefs. Constantly they checked their findings against the revelation of God in their Bible, and the writings of their sages in the Talmud, and against the wisdom of their fathers. Their norms of truth were determined by the Bible, by their experiences, and by their reasons.

In the shtetl the wheels of nature ground slowly, and so did the lives of the Jews. Solitary, stable, shrewd, the shtetl Jew inched his way along from the first prayer in the morning, *"Modeh Ani,"* "I give thanks unto Thee that Thou didst return my soul,"[8] to the last prayer at night, *"K'Rias Shema"* (the saying of the Shema before retiring) added to which were those words: "Tremble and sin not, commune in your heart upon your bed and keep silent, Selah"; from the first holiday of the year *Rosh Hashanah* symbolizing the yearning for the divine gift of redemption, to the last holiday of the year *Tisha B'ab* commemorating the destruction of the Temple. With the same graduation he contrived to forge a strong link between his inspiring past and his dream of the future. He managed to guard zealously his spiritual independence as he went about the business of making a precarious living, rearing his family, keeping his emotions under control and his clenched fists in his pockets.

Interestingly enough, despite the rigidity of traditions, rules, and regulations, shtetl life, in a sense, was quite plastic, even fluid. These Jews had the sensation that they and their culture were continuing phenomena, that there was a certain flow in their existence as they spanned generations. To be sure, the individual passed on and had to be replaced, but the replacement was not merely achieved through reproduction—the learning of the particular ways of Jewish life was vitally essential to the completion of this process. Ordinarily a member of any given group needs only acquaint himself with as much of his cultural environment as is necessary to prepare him to fit into some niche in his society; however, in the case of the Jewish child he needed some very special things because he was to live in a unique group, within a larger group. Generally speaking, man's struggle from the cradle to the grave is to become a mere "human being," but in the shtetl the Jew had the added strain of becoming and staying Jewish. He had to learn to be not only a Russian, a Pole, a Hungarian, or a Lithuanian but also a Russian Jew, or a Polish Jew, or

---

[8] It is interesting to note that this prayer does not contain the name of the Lord because it was given even before one had the chance to wash his hands, and therefore was not "purified."

a Hungarian Jew, or a Lithuanian Jew; and he also had to learn how to behave as one who comes from the "wrong side of the street" (in refined German, *Judenstrasse*).

The shtetl Jews were neither *de jure* nor *de facto* full-fledged citizens of the countries in which they lived. Nor did they, in spirit, feel they were true citizens. As a matter of fact they were not expected to be wholehearted patriots of the countries which treated them like stepchildren, although to the extent which they were permitted to serve such countries, they usually served them loyally. Actually most Jews have been good citizens of their countries because they too often wish to over-compensate for their homelessness—sometimes to the point of poor taste but always to the advantage of their countries.

Naturally their basic concern was with developments (in the country where they existed as a hated and persecuted minority) which would affect their own lives and interests. Step by step this attitude, logical and justified as it was in the light of the treatment accorded them in all those countries, developed a kind of philosophy of Diaspora. It was a philosophy of complete passivism. This nonresistance to evil seems to have served them very well through the centuries. To be sure, non-Jews felt a distaste for this sort of attitude, yet Gandhi practiced it quite successfully, and Jesus himself asked his followers to forgive their enemies, to turn the other cheek and to come in peace. The Jewish outlook on life provided for them an ideological foundation for the sad realities facing mankind in general and Jews in particular. Although they firmly believed that they were an important cog in the play of forces in history, they could not, at this juncture, take an active part in its march across time and space. No matter what happened to them—a pogrom in Russia, an anti-Semitic outburst in Germany, a Dreyfus affair in France—it was all a matter of escaping for the moment, for one could not fight this tide.[9]

[9] People wonder at the strange antics of Jews in Israel as compared to those who cringed and crawled before the Russian police or the Nazi bully. Eric Hoffer, gives what seems like a reasonable explanation: "In Europe the Jew faced his enemies alone, an isolated individual, a speck of life floating in an eternity of Nothingness." In Israel he became quite a formidable force as the Arab nations will attest. There he was reckless, stubborn, and resource-

Poverty, injustice, disease are evils which no optimism can shut out completely, and the shtetl Jews had to endure these conditions. Although they did their best to change them, they could not, so they changed their attitude toward them. This calls for a steadfast conviction, a deep insight, a keen sense of humor, and a vivid imagination.

One must not conclude too hastily that this behavior was a slimy capitulation to fatalism. Let it be said that it was not a compromise of basic values, but rather a fusion of desirables which combined to act for them as a panacea (half tonic, half opiate), an ironic demonstration of a defensive strategy which in the end proved to be a most effective offensive strategy. It is as though they stood there in quicksand and said to the whole world: "Here we are, at this hour, in all of its contingencies, not in some irrecoverable past nor in some wished-for future. Here we are in all our humanity, a living mixture of weakness and strength, sorrow and hope, not in some vague state of being." To function in this sort of awareness of the reality of life made sense against what seemed to them to be a senseless world. They grasped well the dramatic inner meaning that lies in the simultaneous occurrence of diverse things. To be sure, they had cause to wonder how it is that a world created in justice and mercy could itself be so unjust and merciless to them, and how God, the Almighty, who so emphatically called forth from them love, righteousness, and loyalty could, at times, demonstrate the opposite traits. And yet they realized that if God did not have these qualities, who then had the right to have them? These were the painful and stubborn facts of life and they took a sagacious long-term view of them. It must be agreed that such an outlook requires a long, tough, and bitter schooling in the ways of the world and of mankind. Indeed here was the story of Job all over again, plot, cast, and all. Here is a devout spirit shaken by personal suffering and universal distress, a patient man who reaches the point where he questions God's justice

---

ful, "a member of an eternal race, with a universal past behind it and a breathtaking future ahead." Eric Hoffer, *The True Believer* (New York: Mentor Books, New American Library, 1962), 63.

and who is finally answered by God, but in such a way that he is more
perplexed than ever. As G. K. Chesterton puts it: "The riddles of
God are more satisfying than the solutions of man."

Thus the Jews of the shtetl reasoned, and thus they were able to preserve and even enlarge their dignity and integrity despite the conditions that surrounded them. Dignity and integrity, they would have reminded the world at large, cannot be measured by the clock, nor faith
by the yard, nor wisdom by the pound. Also, they reached the conclusion that, because of their position, they owed nothing to any other
group and expected nothing from them, and thus they finally acquired
the habit of considering themselves as standing alone, believing that
their entire destiny was in their own hands, and, furthermore, that
the Jewish history of the future would only be the lengthening shadow
of themselves.

They were certain indeed that Ecclesiastes, the preacher, knew
what he was talking about when he said that "to every thing there
is a season, and a time to every purpose under the heaven" (3:1) and
that the "race is not to the swift, nor the battle to the strong" (9:11).

And so, whereas the drive for survival seems to be innate and subconscious in most people, in the case of the Jews it was also conscious, deliberate, and planned, so that fate which had taken care of
them so long would somehow continue to save them.

To the outsider the shtetl was ever incomprehensible, just as to the
ones inside it was quite comprehensible. This is understandable
since only one who has experienced, on the one hand, the shattering
disillusionment and the shocking anxiety of living in such a social atmosphere, and on the other hand the blessedness, the inspiration, the
sense of destiny emanating from God's revelation, could conceive the
real meaning of this sort of life—a life which was more than creed.
Rather it was a formula for serving God and men and satisfying the
needs of life.

There are some hardheaded empiricists who would insist that the
shtetl was a mystical phenomenon and not a scientific fact. They
argue, and with a great deal of validity, that to admit any dimension
or order other than the physical is to abandon all the progress man

has made since he began to close the doors to ignorance, superstition, and mythology. The shtetl Jews would answer them with some questions: So far so good, but is there a scale in physics to weigh the inspiration of the twenty-third Psalm? Is there a set of numbers in mathematics to measure the beauty of the Song of Songs? Is there a formula in chemistry to analyze the nature of the strength to be found in the Shema?

There are many others who sincerely believe that this self-isolation, this self-chosen people concept, even the passion for survival against all odds, was merely a neurotic form of collective egoism. But the shtetl Jews were convinced that they had the right idea and that they possessed textual proof for their point of view, truth which had traveled from the broad expanse of the Haran desert to every muddy street in the shtetl and from the heights of majestic Mt. Sinai to the humblest shack on that street. And, furthermore, they were also convinced that the smaller the outside world tried to make them, the greater they appeared to themselves.

As a matter of fact, no conceivable discipline was better calculated to breed the strength and courage needed by this group to survive, for out of their shattering experience they were able to face life with new confidence. Indeed, they stripped their lives of nonessentials, they earned their kopecs, ate their bread, drank their tea, said their prayers, and wrapped themselves in their holy shawls as though to keep out the cold of intolerance, the wind of persecution, and the rain of hate.

How in the world could any outsider understand the strange behavior of those people whose motto was ever before them, written by an invisible hand: "Your yesterday is your present, your today is your future, and your tomorrow is your secret."

To the individual, Jewishness meant "my way of life in which religion, values, social structure, individual behavior are inextricably blended."[10] The word describing this feeling was *yiddishkeit*, a word charged with joy and pride, despite the frightening responsi-

[10] Zborowski and Herzog, *Life Is with People*, 428.

bilities that went with it. These responsibilities sometimes seemed all but overwhelming, for, despite the strength and inspiration, hope and dreams of shtetl life there was little peace. One could say with Jeremiah (6:14): "Peace, peace; when there is no peace." Although these Jews could not eat or drink, or pray or play with their non-Jewish neighbors, they did have to buy from them, sell to them, rent from them, live near them, be bullied and persecuted by them, cursed and beaten by them, burned by them, and made to feel alone in the world by them. This aloneness was not like the pleasant state of being alone as one feels as he sits alone by his fireplace on a winter evening. This aloneness is much like the aloneness of birth and death. It is the aloneness one sees in the eyes of one who is suffering deeply and helplessly. The Jews of the shtetl had a strong suspicion that their Gentile neighbors, instead of raising themselves to a higher level by more creative and socially useful work, attempted to achieve superiority by lowering the prestige of the Jews. It has been said that "passionate hatred can give meaning and purpose to an empty life." Those antisocial, destructive proclivities were idealized, glorified, and fostered by the church leaders. They stirred up the Russian peasants to the point of blind fury and hatred against the helpless Jews—these peasants who lived on the rugged edges of a society which kept them submerged, hungry, cold, superstitious, frustrated, and forever wallowing about not only in mud but in religious sentiment as well.

The basis for the vicious anti-Semitism surrounding the shtetl was religion, and it generated a most fanatical and deep-seated attitude which manifested itself in the worst sort of terrifying persecution. Except in the matter of degree there was little difference between the Holy Offices of the Inquisition, the torture chambers of the Third Reich, and the treatment dealt out by the vultures of prejudice, hate, and greed who encircled the Jews in the shtetl.

Anti-Semitism is a recurrent and universal phenomenon which disturbs students of human nature even though it defies complete sociological analysis. Actually it is a tangled and complex cultural occurrence—illogical, inconsistent, exaggerated, base, and horrible, but glaringly and painfully real. In the words of Morris Raphael Cohen:

"Anti-Semitism is not instinctive, though it may appear so to the unreflecting. Nor is it due to unalterable traits any more than to unalterable divine decree. No single factor can adequately explain such a complex human phenomenon. It arises from a mixture of diverse historical factors, religious, economic and political, coupled with ignorance and prejudice, just like other problems which vex human society."[11] This remains certain: prejudice in general and anti-Semitism in particular is a phenomenon originating wholly in the mind, and the human mind is a curious instrument. It is a great deal like the sea, possessing deeps and shallows, cold, dark profundities as well as sunny crests. Responsible psychologists, sociologists, and psychiatrists all agree that prejudice is the tendency to transfer guilt and blame from person to person and from group to group. The causes of prejudice are frustration, guilt, fear, anxiety, and need for self-glorification. When we persecute a minority group we project on them the burden of our own sins and by punishing them we hope to expiate our own sense of guilt. The action of the world around the shtetl is a classic example of this phenomenon.

The story of man, the religious animal, is full of contradictions—some beautiful, some tragic, some funny, some ugly, all illuminating; and here is a glaring example of this strange ambivalence in the Christian soul which enables it to hold the cross in one hand and the sword in the other. The Christians of the shtetl days had what they believed to be a rather good authority for their outlook. Pope Innocent III himself repeated the accusation that Jews secretly murdered Christians and held that Jews were under the curse of God and condemned to serfdom. He forbade their appearance on the streets at Easter, he authorized their payment of an annual tax to the church, and he deprived them of public office. Pontius Pilate even became a hero and was immortalized by the Apostles' Creed. He and his wife were transformed into Christians and thereupon into saints. Every year, on June 25, the Ethiopian Christian church commemorates the sainthood of the Pilates.

[11] Morris Raphael Cohen, *Reflections of a Wondering Jew* (Boston: Beacon Press, 1950), 116.

Jews have long wondered how it is that Christianity, which seems so preoccupied with matters of humanity, could be so intolerant in regard to the Jews. The conclusion they must have reached is that when Christians are occupied with humanity they forget the Jews, and that when they are occupied with the Jews they forget humanity.

The people of the shtetl believed that the Christians' argument regarding the irreligiosity and the damnation of the Jews generated more heat than light and more passion than reason; that the Christians' hatred sprang, essentially, from their self-contempt; and that their fervent chauvinism and religious enthusiasm often served them as a refuge from a guilty conscience.[12]

The shtetl Jews pooh-poohed the whole idea of their responsibility for the crucifixion of Jesus. They refused to consider themselves guilty of deicide. How, they argued, can any human being kill a God, since God is above and beyond human reach and surely beyond the ability of human beings to destroy? In fact, they were convinced that anti-Semitism has never been a true religious issue at all but an excuse used by people to cover up their inner hate, their passion for power, their emotional need for intolerance, and their justification for greed. History made it plain to them that Jesus was born among Jews, in a Jewish community, and his message was for Jews alone. From beginning to end Christianity was a Jewish phenomenon; it sprang from the bosom of Judaism, it was nurtured by Jews, and Judaism has influenced it ever since. In truth, many Jews have secretly regretted letting it get away from them, realizing that much tragedy would have been prevented if it had not been rejected.

It is the opinion of this writer that the ancient Jews brought forth a genius and did not know what to do with him, which is usually the case where geniuses are concerned. It was and is today a delicate and awkward situation for both Jews and Christians. The Jews could

---

[12] "Such an injustice as that done by the Gentile church to Judaism is almost unprecedented in the annals of history. The Gentile church stripped it of everything, she took away its sacred books; herself a transformation of Judaism, she cut off all connection with the parent religion. The daughter first robbed her mother and then repudiated her." Conrad Henry Moehlman, *The Christian-Jewish Tragedy* (New York: Leo Hart, 1933), 211.

not in good conscience accept Jesus as their Messiah, and the Christians have yet to show any gratitude to the Jews for producing their Messiah. As a matter of fact, Christians resent the Jews because they gave truth to Jesus, and hate them for having discovered him. This whole business is a sociopsychological *mishmash*, if there ever was one.

Jews would have liked to view Jesus himself as one who possessed a winning gentleness, which arose from his own humility and from his deep faith in his fellow man, and a perfect equanimity proceeding from his profound trust in God; however, his followers, by their unmistakable behavior have discouraged this.

As far as the Christian passion to convert Jews is concerned, the attitude of the average Jew toward this conduct was and is now not only one of moral aversion but of intellectual incompatibility. Actually, the shtetl Christians were not overly concerned—Jews had no souls to save. The persecution of Jews by Christians over the centuries has made it impossible for any but a tiny minority of Jews to accept the Christian answer that the Old Testament found its fulfillment in Jesus the Messiah. Here is one of the major sins of the Christian church.[13]

No matter the attitude Jews had or now have about Jesus, they cannot overlook the value of Jesus and his teachings from the point of view of universal history. Joseph Klausner sums up this feeling: "And if the day should come when the ethical core of Jesus be stripped of its wrappings of miracles and mysticism, it will be one of the choicest treasures in the literature of Israel for all time."[14]

The average Jew of the shtetl, however, had neither the time nor the inclination to get involved in much of this sort of mental gymnastics. Most of the time he merely looked about him, shook his head, and wondered about that strange God of his. On the one hand He directs the stars in their heavenly courses, and on the other hand He

[13] Gabriel Hebert, *The Old Testament from Within* (London: Oxford University Press, 1962), 123.

[14] Joseph Klausner, *Jesus of Nazareth* (New York: Macmillan Co., 1957), 413.

gives drunken peasants the strength to beat, burn, and murder innocent men, women, and children whose only sin was being born into
a Jewish family. And yet Jews had no other choice, since there was
only this one God. Where else could they go but to Him? "Yea,
though He slay me, yet will I trust in Him," was not only the triumphant answer given by Job in his bitter fate, but it has been the persistent answer given to life by the Jewish prophets and teachers, and
the little man throughout the ages.

So the church leaders, the Czarist puppets, together with the
Muziks, contrived to make life unbearable for the Jews. Indeed, they
would manage to have the shtetl Jews crippled and then blame them
for limping. Max Nordau once explained this situation very well in
a straightforward and succinct fashion when he said: "Jews are not
hated because they have evil qualities, evil qualities are sought for
in them because they are hated."

There were times when fearful apprehension seized them that un-
righteousness would triumph in the end and hatred prove to be the
permanent way of life, when it seemed indeed that their God was
slumbering in His heaven for long periods of time. There must have
been moments when the impossible resolve suggested itself to them—
make peace with this insane world, surrender to it, give up your
ideals and inspirations, dreams and hopes. Yet somehow during those
dark moments most of them turned to the Psalmist who reminded
them: "Behold, He who keeps Israel will neither slumber nor sleep . . .
the Lord will keep your going out and your coming in from this time
forth and for evermore." They turned to the Torah and remembered
the promises, "Ye are a kingdom of priests," and "I will make of
thee a great nation." And in their prayer book are the words: "Behold, happy is the man whom God correcteth, therefore despise not
thou the chastening of the Almighty: For He maketh sore, and bind-
eth up: He woundeth, and His hands make whole." And these beliefs and the strength they created became a bridge between their
heritage of yesterday and the hope of tomorrow, a heritage which,
for generations, had generated their purpose in the world, had kept
their conscience burning within them, and had kept awake their

longing for a way of life based on the brotherhood of man and the fatherhood of God.

Gerald Abrahams suggests a most novel and an entirely new definition for Judaism which is apropos at this point. He says: "Psychologically, Jew-hate breeds an antibody which is the Jewish obsession. Few Jews are without this. Indeed it is a factor that suggests a definition: Jewry is not a race, a religion, but an obsession—an anxiety neurosis."[15]

So each Jew in the shtetl became a prophet in his heart and did his best to believe what is written in Leviticus: "In righteousness shall you judge your neighbor." But they paid the price for their long look backwards, whence they came and why, for their unflinching assessment of the present, and they went slowly into the future with Hosea who had said to them: "Come and let us return unto the Lord: for He hath torn, and He will heal us; He hath smitten, and He will bind us up" (6:1). And they continued "to think otherwise," and they still dared to go into the darkness about them, and passionate devoutness still remained the answer to the ignorance and intolerance around them. That Jews were idealistic in those dark days was singularly fortunate for Judaism. There was great need for idealism to leaven the cruel and wretched realism of that period in man's history.

Thus they continued to live in a sort of "duoverse" rather than a universe, and both were very real to them. In a period in which symbolism and fantasy have become more and more important and in which any sophomore in college can talk about levels of meaning, it may seem strange that for those in the shtetl there were basically only two levels of meaning—the one dealing with their outer universe and the one dealing with their inner universe. As far as the denizens of the outer universe were concerned, they possessed a thanalistic outlook about the shtetl—to know it was to destroy it. The average non-Jew felt uncomfortably aware of his lack of understanding of the Jews and his lack of control over Jewish behavior. He really did not know who the Jews were, and tended to lump them as a group, *sui generis*.

[15] Gerald Abrahams, *The Jewish Mind* (Boston: Beacon Press, 1961), 32.

He knew little about their strange ways, how they lived, where they came from, what they wanted from life, or where they were going. The Jews, in turn, had no confidence in the world around them. To them it was a world of ignorance and superstition, pain and trouble. There was no protection out there from barbarous physical violence and no hope for social betterment, not only for them but for any ordinary human being. So they retreated into their own world, a world of things of the spirit, but also a world of "arid wilderness of ceremonial law, the barren hypersubleties of Talmudic debate, the dead-sea fruit of learning, unquickened by living water."[16]

The people of the shtetl, while standing with bowed heads before the local policeman, priest, or noble, considered power, glory, and authority as of little significance because they were fully aware that they themselves stood far above those individuals in matters of moral behavior, spiritual strength, and dreams of a decent world for all man. Being subservient would appear to most people to be degrading and insulting, yet the shtetl Jews found it to be a refuge of the philosopher; and, properly carried out, it proved to be a position of power, strange as it may seem. "Exodus" was their battle cry—it aroused the inert, it shook up the backslider, it generated hope, it gathered strength, it took on new purpose, and fiercely made them aware of life's reality.

Despite the attitude of the outside world the Jew of the shtetl was a necessary evil there—he was needed for economic reasons (Jews carried on most of the petty but necessary trading in the community) as well as for psychic reasons. As a matter of fact, it was Bismarck who once admitted that " if we had no Jews in Germany we would have to import them." One suspects that Hitler had the same sentiments. Thus the shtetl Jews reacted to the outside world in a utilitarian manner. They surely did not consider their behavior as having to do with some sort of philosophical "schema" but rather as a feature of everyday, down to earth living.[17] Thus understood, utili-

---

[16] Israel Zangwill, *Dreamers of the Ghetto* (New York: Bloch Publishing Co., 1923), 224.

[17] If the writer will be permitted a personal allusion, he would like to tell of an experience he once had in relation to the term "utilitarian." Years ago the writer went to Mexico, to study cultural anthropology, and in order to

tarianism is a tendency to exact from every moment of life a positive yield in action. This is not to imply that all these Jews were selfish— it was rather a group reaction, resulting from fortuitous circumstances. It was inevitable that in so strange and unprecedented an environment would arise this sort of outlook. In any event, it carried them through deep emotional storms and unheavals, it helped them to penetrate every sham of their time and gave particular, significant meaning to their unique experience. Indeed, it can be said that human motives are curiously mixed and human behavior rarely consistent.

In his book *The Slave* Isaac Bashevis Singer, considered by many the most brilliant living representative of the Yiddish language in prose and one of the greatest Yiddish writers of all time, recreates beautifully life in the shtetl with all of its pettiness, intolerance, and vicious gossip, as well as the pain, fear, and humiliation experienced by its members in their life struggle.[18]

That world was thrifty, parsimonious, intensely local. The people were desperately poor, restricted in occupation, burdened by heavy taxes, packed together in crowded quarters, sometimes accused of using Christian blood in their rituals, desecrating the host, and poisoning wells. The writer recalls painfully well the Beilis affair in 1913. Mendal Beilis was accused of having murdered a twelve-year-old Christian boy whose blood was to be used for ritual purposes during the Passover festival. The trial took place in Kiev and was used by the Russian officials, the anti-Semitic clergymen, and the press to stir up anti-Jewish riots throughout the country. Beilis was eventually cleared, but during the trial the Jews of Russia lived in constant fear

---

be able to visit and stay in many of the hinterland communities he had to make special arrangements. He was completing several forms, and in answer to the inquiry regarding religion he wrote "Jewish." The gentleman in charge of the program in the New Orleans office stared at the word "Jewish" and stated without any fanfare that "this will never do." The writer answered that, in fact, he had another religious preference, he was a *Utilitarian*. The Mexican official accepted this, and the writer spent many months in Mexico as a member of the First Utilitarian Church of Lafayette.

[18] Isaac Bashevis Singer, *The Slave* (New York: Farrar, Straus, and Cudahy, 1962).

and trepidation. Jews were forever being accused of having an aversion to manual labor, an antipathy to science and worldliness, a preference for trade and a love of money. Moses Mendelsohn once answered this accusation very well: "People continue to keep us away from all contacts with the arts and science, or with trades and occupations which are useful and have dignity. They bar all roads leading to increased usefulness and then use our lack of culture to justify our continued oppression. They tie our hands and then reproach us that we do not use them. . . ."[19] The shtetl Jews had a more immediate answer. There was scant room in the rigid system of their life for outside concern and mere academic thinking. The stern demands of necessity held them in their grip, narrowing the horizon of their minds and obscuring the outside world, forcing them to hold on to ancient habits and traditions.

Indeed, the shoemaker should stick to his last and the baker to his bread and the rabbi to his Torah. Their stomachs may have been filled with boiled potatoes and baked herring but their minds were crammed with the riches of the Talmud, the wisdom of Solomon, the poetry of David, and the directives of Moses.

They were also accused of being physically incompetent and in the shtetl they were particularly reproved for their weakness of physical force. Those Jews learned early to despise physical strength but to care about the power of the spirit; thus they never felt inferior in matters of physical endeavor. In general, Jews believe that combat, be it in the rough and tumble of sports or in the dreadfulness of war, is a primitive pastime and serves to fulfill the role of an emotional outlet for the primitive cravings of modern man.

For a long time Jews have demonstrated a trait that Dr. Erich Fromm calls "biophilia" (love of life). A biophilous person "wants to mold and influence by love, by reason, and by his example."[20] He loves the adventure of living, and his approach to life is functional

[19] Simon Noveck (ed.), *Great Personalities in Modern Times* (Washington: B'nai B'rith Department of Adult Jewish Education, 1965), 24.
[20] Erich Fromm, "Creators and Destroyers," XLVII, *Saturday Review* (January 4, 1964), 22.

rather than mechanical. To him, God is reverence for life and all that enhances life. It is this author's opinion that such a trait is not inborn but developed as the result of socialization. These people live for the future. The opposite type, Dr. Fromm calls "necrophilous." This group is concerned more with death, which excites and satisfies them; they worship force and are sadistic in their outlook. The biophilous attitude has been a powerful force in the lives of Jews. It has civilized them, but also it has been responsible for their lack of interest in purely physical strength. They kept remembering that it was written: "They shall beat their swords into plowshare and their spears into pruning hooks; nation shall not lift up sword against nation, neither shall they learn war anymore" (Isa., 2:4).[21] Because of this view of life Jews have ever exalted the abstract, the spiritual, and the intellectual above the physical and the sensate. They have placed the "book" above the "sword." The shtetl Jews would not have for one moment agreed with Nietzsche, the progenitor of Hitler's philosophy of Aryan superiority and the "superman-übermensch," who tried so tragically to create a climate in which the "strong, beautiful beast" would rule the world. To be sure, the Jews paid a dear price for their stubbornness with six million lives.

It is interesting to note that, in general, Jews do not care very much even for the sports of hunting and fishing. They have an aversion for guns, and they somehow fail to get a thrill out of killing which gives so many people a sense of superiority. Even today we find few Jews excelling in sports; there are very few Jews in professional sports.[22]

In the drama which was played in the shtetl as the stage, there appeared saints and sinners, good men and scoundrels, *shnorers* and generous people, loyal individuals and informers, pious men and apostates, heroes and cowards. But most of them were heroes—albeit to the outside world they may have appeared as tragic heroes—and

[21] There have been times when Jews could show a certain type of strength as the story of the Maccabee brothers, and the experiences of the Nazis around the Warsaw ghetto, and of the Arabs around the Negev will attest.

[22] Harold U. Ribalow does a fine job discussing this topic in *The Jew in American Sports* (New York: Bloch Publishing Co., 1959).

"tragic heroes" seems to be a contradiction in terms, a failure by definition. However, the tragedy depends on the conviction that the hero in his failure is still more than ever nobler than those about him. The feeling about such a hero is not warranted by his great accomplishment but rather by his outstanding effort in the business of uncompromising courage under the sting of everyday living.

There was very little of the idea of social classes in the shtetl. Every Jew there learned early in life that in order to survive each must work for the other man, each must help to carry the other man's burden. They grasped the realities of life firmly enough to be able to believe that although the Jew with the Shema on his lips is surely one of God's creatures, it is equally true that the drunken Russian peasant is also one of His creatures.

There was no affectation of "blue blood" among those Jews although theirs was a pedigree which made a joke of the royalty of Europe, the nobility of British society, and the aristocracy of Christian churchianity. If they had any concept of aristocracy it was of one made up of the learned, the teacher, the sage. As a matter of fact, from the time of Joachanan ben Zakkai, after the temple was destroyed, a new type of man became the idol of the Jews, not the man of wealth or the powerful athlete, but the scholar. Indeed, if there were an upper class among them it was not of birth, wealth, or power but of learning often to the point of marked evil. The scholars began to grow proud and vain. They looked on the am ha-åretz, the man of the soil, the working man, with disdain.

The quest for meaning was for the shtetl Jews foredoomed. To be sure they had their own two feet to stand on and their own human trinity, as it were—reason, courage, grace—but these were not enough to see them through. They needed something else; they needed a faith and an optimism, which in their case stemmed from their belief in God and their belief in man—thus they believed in themselves, in their neighbors, and in all mankind. It is as though while they were slushing through the filth, the mud, and the snow of the community's street they were climbing a ladder.

No matter what anyone else thought, to the shtetl Jews their credo did not seem a mere distillate, or abstract, desiccated element, but something as rich and as concrete as the most positive and practical experience one could have. To them the wisdom of Solomon was clear: "God created man to be immortal and made him to be an image of His own eternity. The souls of the righteous are in the hands of God, and there shall no torment touch them. . . . For even if in the might of men they be punished, their hope is full of immortality, and having borne a little chastening they shall receive a great good."[23]

This sort of outlook kept a fresh breeze blowing into the windows of the shtetl and into the corners of the Jews' stale existence. With them the commonplace routine had a touch of their audacity; they believed they could pull anything out of their hats, even greatness. What they really wanted was that the world be once again restored to them, so that they might break bread in peace again with their families, drink tea in the morning without fear, read the prayerbook in the evening, and sleep without having to awake from nightmare to nightmare. But this world was not restored to them, and they accepted their slices of life as they did their slices of black bread on weekdays and the slices of *challah* on the Sabbath with one eye directed toward the universal future and the other toward the narrowness of their everyday life.

In the shtetl the one great miracle was the daily rebirth of God in the individual soul; every new day was a resurrection of the spirit, every act a fresh wonder; faith, hope, and inspiration would take them through the next twenty-four hours. They were far more interested in God than in Caesar (from which comes the word "Czar"). When Caesar tried to impose his will on them they quietly went about the business of ignoring him and followed their own ways unto the Lord.

Oddly enough, although in many ways the shtetl Jews were slaves, yet to some extent there they were their own masters. Indeed, in some respects they were even more their own masters than have Jews been in free countries. There at least they led lives which were

[23] Joseph Herman Hertz (ed.), *The Voice of Prayer: A Book of Thoughts* (New York: Bloch Publishing Co., 1943), 200.

distinctly their own and, despite the poverty, political insecurity, and brutal intolerance, they felt deep convictions and were, strangely enough, psychically strong and spiritually secure.

Thus those skullcap apostles of religious freedom, of social justice, of personal liberty, of human equality; those men, women, and children of courage and mischief, of warmth and humor; those tragic heroes of history spent their lives waiting from birth to death as most people do but with this important difference—they knew what they were waiting for. At every step—at the work of their calling, at their meals, at their prayers, at their talmudic arguments, at home or away, from morning until late in the evening, from youth to old age, consciously or unconsciously—they went about the business of creating the springtime of Judaism as it was to become defined throughout the world.

And the echo of the shtetl's voice was ever the same: "No doubt, but ye are the people."

V

No Doubt but Ye Are the People

Shema Yisroel'—"Hear O Israel," spoke the Lord to the men, women, and children of the shtetl. "Ye are the people." And the people answered: *"El Kelohanu"*—"There is none like our God." And God laid a finger on the brow of each of them and reminded them that the "secret things belong to the Lord but those things which are revealed belong unto you and your children forever that you may do all the words of the law."

These things which were revealed constitute the Jews' unifying sweep of ideas. By the breadth and sharpness of their minds, by the warmth of their spirits, and by their adeptness at compromise they were able to crystallize these things into a philosophy of life—a formula for living. Indeed, these things became the substance of their collective soul. And these drab, cowed figures of the shtetl measured the outside world, sized it up carefully and rejected it, and went back into their extremely limited world filled with squalor and pain, but which they knew and where they could hold on to their apocalyptic dream of the future. This milieu transformed their spirits into a deeply felt consciousness of being and provided them with a place and a name. They were content to follow this star until brighter ones came along. However, for the time being, they were equally concerned with a negative desire, that of learning to stay where they

were. The Jews of the shtetl seemed to have had the rare capacity
to bear a great deal of reality.

To attempt to describe such a people is like attempting to describe
a sound. One may hear it, feel it, and perhaps, through the marvel
of modern gadgetry, see it and take a picture of it, but to describe it
is practically impossible.

It is fascinating as it is unbelievable how heavily an undertaking
such as this leans on one's memory—small things in themselves, but
bearing a most provocative magic. Suddenly fifty years turn back
and a scene is for one hour reborn. Carried in the subconscious are
strangely unrelated moments, the queer odor of dirty snow, the mel-
ancholy beat of a bird at twilight, the painful yelp of a dog in the distance, the fear of Russian peasants banging on the door, the honking
of geese on the meadow, the musty smell of the *shul* (synagogue),
the one-room wooden hut muttering to itself in the night, the warmth
of the big brick oven in the kitchen, the deep attachment for a little
old grandmother in a peruke, the bright, rounded faces of younger
brothers, the superhuman strength of a brave mother, the nearness of
God on the Sabbath—they have no connection but they come together, solitary wanderers, at the chance meeting of this hour in this
bright study ten thousand miles away.

How does one go about describing people who seemed to have been
suspended between two levels—the wet, gray *potzel* soil under their
feet and the long, impassioned dream of heaven above their heads?
It is nearly as futile as calling today's sunrise modern, or disengaging
a spider web made of fine silken threads, or grasping the psyche by
going into one's mortal body.

How does one examine a people who lived more in time than in
space? "It was as if their soul was always on the way, as if the secret
of their heart had no affinity with things. . . . He was a unique kind
of man, the shtetl Jew, who possessed a unique kind of charm, a
charm which came from the inner richness of their being."[1]

How does one analyze a people who, for the time being, were

[1] Heschel, *The Earth Is the Lord's*, 15

standing once more in the land of Moab, between Horeb and the land of Canaan, with the possession of the promised land only begun, not completed?

What sort of critique can one offer of a people whose *Nahalah* (inheritance) came directly from God Himself? "For thou art an holy people unto the Lord thy God: the Lord thy God hath chosen thee to be a special people unto himself, above all people that are upon the face of the earth" (Deut. 7:6).

How does one evaluate a group of people who believed that they could define God, who would have laughed at St. Augustine's observation that "we can know what God is not but we cannot know what he is"? They knew what He is. They had traveled over a great deal of slippery ground to find out. They knew God personally, so personally that, in their sense of humor, they tried with considerable skill and effort to outwit Him. Indeed, they needed to offer no proof that they knew Him because their experience did away with need of proof. Proof rests only upon experience, and their experience throughout history speaks for itself. This is certain: what happened between the people of the shtetl and God did not happen in a vacuum—it happened in their shule, on their streets, in their homes, every day as well as on the Sabbath, while they were eating, sleeping, studying, working.

In the light of this writer's unique experience, his years of participation and observation, and his sociological training, he is going to judge them and analyze them with his heart, flavored with imagination, bolstered by intuition, and driven by memory.

Many will be justly critical of this approach which offers so little weight of "statistical evidence"; however, it may be possible that the writer, like Balaam's donkey, can see things others cannot see. Balaam was a very influential man, so important that the king of Moab sent for him to come, personally, in order that he might curse Israel. Balaam saddled his nondescript little donkey and went to meet Balaki, king of Moab. But the Lord sent an angel to prevent him, and the angel took a stand across the path of Balaam and his mount, and

Balaam, though a man of wisdom and discernment, could not see the angel of the Lord, but the little donkey could.

What appears to one person as a delirious imbecility can appear to another to be axiomatic, clear, and certain as the stars in the heavens above. What I am suggesting, then, is that this sort of awareness may come nearest to breathing life into these people who for so long have been shadows, and to presenting the reality behind the truth in the fibre of their days, years, generations, and ages spent in the shtetl.

It is a fact of human existence that man has ever been enmeshed in the boundless quest for knowledge about himself, his relationship with his God and his neighbors, and the environment in which he must live. The knowledge he has gathered about these areas of life together make up his philosophy of living. It is a most elementary truism that philosophies of life cannot be conjured up out of thin air. A great number of highly complex and dynamic forces are responsible for an outlook on life no matter how simple the society may be. This especially applies in the case of the shtetl people. In order to live with the near and with the far, with the day's menial and petty tasks and with the yearnings for the future, they went back to the ideas, ideals, laws, and commandments of their forefathers, which they considered as God's own testimony, and bound them together into a pattern of living, strict and clear-cut, which defined for them the meaning of every element in their individual and collective life. If anyone should question their inability to "change" they would simply quote Ecclesiastes the preacher who said (1:10): "Is there a thing thereof it is said 'See, It is new?' It hath been already in the ages which were before us." Their loyalty to this way of life was a consuming passion; it enabled them to tuck the horizon of their microcosm closely around them like a blanket and defy the biting winds of the outside world. In the face of the frustrations, defeats, constant pressures, the people of the shtetl developed, through time, a social system which was apparently well adjusted to their needs in that alien setting.

Thus it was that the traditional Jewish code of behavior formed a

logical, integrated law which served as a standard for personal conduct and at the same time as an unwritten ordinance for the entire
group. In other words, their "constitution" might read this way:
"Cultivate the Jewish way and you and all of Judaism will have happiness, peace, and security." It must also be noted correspondingly,
that, the "chosen people" must be judged by stricter standards than
other people. "You only have I known of all the families of the
earth: therefore I will punish you for all your iniquities." (Amos
3:2) The people of the shtetl were the chosen of God; therefore, it
is He only who may judge them, but they will remain chosen only if
they practice righteousness, justice, mercy, and walk humbly with
Him.

In spite of the many outside influences that the Jewish "way" absorbed and the changes it underwent in many localities and in the
course of many centuries, the specifically Jewish components in the
folk life of Jews everywhere had biblical and talmudic origins. In
the shtetl particularly, a tendency developed among its people to conduct their entire lives, including all daily and periodic activities, in
conformity with explicit or implicit rules. These latter are contained
either in the Writ or in oral tradition, and are known as the *Halakha*;
the legends, poetry, and philosophic sayings together are called the
Haggadah. This religious tradition became the main molding force
of Judaism with all its customs and usages.

According to an ancient Hebrew saying, the world rests upon three
pillars—learning, worship, and charity. "Learning," as Rabbi Abraham Heschel has pointed out, "meant having a share in divine wisdom, the object of worship was the creator of heaven and earth; charity meant both openness to and active sympathy for our fellow man's
suffering."[2]

Each person in the shtetl believed that, whether he was standing
squarely on these pillars or merely hanging on, these pillars constituted the foundation of his entire social group and that the measure
of all existence carried, as a result, the full range of responsibility and

[2] Abraham Joshua Heschel, White House Conference on Children and
Youth, 1960.

choice of one's behavior. To balance this sort of egocentrism each person had to reflect often with David the Psalmist: "When I consider thy heavens, the work of thy hands, the moon and the stars, which thou hast made; What is man, that thou are mindful of him?" (Psalms 8:3, 4). But there were these words to console him: "Thou hast made him but a little lower than the angels." Indeed, man might on the one hand, be the most miserable of beings; yet, on the other hand, he was the creation of God and possessed certain rights, dignities, and graces of his own. Thus God spread His wings over the shtetl, ever reminding each person that, since he was made in God's image, he could fulfill God's purpose only with his entire life, with body, mind, and spirit, yet hinting strongly that God did not really need man to fulfill His purposes; it is rather that God willed to have the help of man.

One of the basic tenets of Judaism has ever been that God is concerned about the common life of man—that He is as much "concerned with the Ethiopian as with the Jew." In the shtetl this concept took on special meaning. The Jews there did not conceive of God merely as a spiritual entity which has no being except in the mind of him who thinks this, but as a reality independent of human thinking and human existence. To be sure, they could not conceive of seeing God any more than the most skilled ophthalmologist can get a glimpse of the soul when he opens the human eye, yet they believed that there is one umbilical cord that can never be cut—the cord which ties each man to his Maker. Thus, God stood in a living relationship to the people of the shtetl and they in the living relationship to him. They were convinced that, whether one accepted Him or not, He was there and that was that—for did He not say to Moses, "I am that I am," when Moses asked Him who and what He was? In short, He was and is *"Melech Chaim,"* the "King of Life."

The shtetl Jews' intimacy with God was startling; it is matched only in a few other religious groups. It was sharpened almost to impertinence, and they spoke to Him as people in no other religion dared to do—such was their relationship to Him. Indeed, they ar-

gued with Him, they chided Him, they bargained with Him, and often
their expressions were expressions of anguish, frenzy, despair, frustration, as well as of hope and adoration. No matter what the argument, it was always cradled within the hands of the Psalmist: "My
soul thirsteth for God, for the living God." This was the eternal expression of the yearning of man for something beyond himself, and
the debate always ended with the thought: "*Im Yiiyeh Ha Shem*"
(God willing).

In trying to answer the question "To what shall we attribute 'the
peculiar religious genius' of the Hebrews?" which Father John L.
McKenzie, s.j., poses in his scholarly and thought-provoking book
The Two-Edged Sword, he suggests that it is essentially the easy
familiarity with the Deity few men have ever been able to enjoy.
"And this easy familiarity was the basis of the Hebrew belief, for the
Lord made Himself known to His people through the patriarchs;
they felt themselves the heirs of the promises which he made to Abraham, Isaac, Jacob, and Moses."[3]

By virtue of this hereditary faculty, Israel was selected to be the
people of prophecy, and every Jew possesses, at least partially, this
gift and hence is capable of the highest religious attainment. But this
faculty, like all other inherited characteristics, is influenced by nurture and by physical environment.[4]

Jews of the shtetl, one and all, believed that indeed they were
particularly blessed with this faculty which generated for them a powerful religious consciousness. They were convinced that to know
God meant to know that He was just, righteous, merciful, considerate,
long-suffering and indestructible, and that the best way to express
their God was by participating in Him.

When the Jew of the shtetl murmured the word *Gotenyu*, be it at
the moment of great joy or at the moment of deep sorrow, he was
pouring out his very heart and soul. It is a term which defies defini-

[3] John L. McKenzie, s.j., *The Two-Edged Sword* (Milwaukee: Bruce Publishing Co., 1955), 26.
[4] Isidor Epstein, *Judaism: A Historical Presentation* (Baltimore: Penguin
Books, 1959), 206.

tion.[5] Yet one who grew up in that environment does not need to have it defined. It is a most comprehensive concept, including the depth and breadth of the spirit, the essence of hurt and pain, the dream of heavenly bliss; it contains the warmth of the morning sunshine and the gloom of the evening shadow, it is the symbol of Judaism's past, the inspiration of its present, and the hope of its future. It implies at the same time a deep reverence for the Almighty as well as the intimacy of two lifelong friends who may disagree at times yet who trust and love each other deeply. In short, the people of the shtetl felt that they were partners with God and thus had a winning combination.[6]

There were many ways in which these men, women, and children could make contact with God: there was prayer, revelation, and miracles. They believed that God is ever present among dedicated groups and may be reached through rituals at the shul and in the home, as well as "when thou walkest by the way, when thou liest down, and when thou risest up."

Thus it was that every child born in a shtetl home soon realized that Judaism was standing outside his door and urging itself upon him, struggling to find a home within him and to direct his actions. Every child in the shtetl aged fast. Reading Torah is not mere theology and dogma—it is, rather, a broad program of education which etches itself deeply into one's entire being. Geographically, the child soon found himself in Canaan, Egypt, Palestine, and Babylon. Historically, he had seen nations come and go; theologically, he had witnessed mighty religions born and fade away; sociologically, he had

---

[5] It is indeed strange that we know exactly what we mean until we try to define it. Translation from one language to another is, at best, difficult. One has to sacrifice either the flavor of a term or its meaning. One French wit explained it this way: "Translations are like women. When they are beautiful they are not faithful and when they are faithful they are not beautiful." There is simply no word in any language that approximates *Gotenyu*. It is a sort of contagious element which captivates the speaker as well as the "listener."

[6] This author recalls vividly the last few words spoken to him by his maternal grandmother as he, his mother, and two brothers drove away in a wagon from their one-room house in Rechicha to begin their escape from Russia. She said: "Benyomen, don't forget God, no matter what you find in America."

learned the bitter story of prejudice, persecution, war, social movement. He read the poetry of David, the wisdom of Solomon, and the
philosophy of Isaiah. He became a linguist, too, for he studied Hebrew, he knew Russian, and he spoke Yiddish.

The shtetl Jews learned quickly that mere profession of a faith is
not enough. In order to be effective, religion must mean great
strength, courage, and inspiration to the individual, but it must also
mean learning to do things a certain way, living with others in deep
sympathy and understanding, and working with them cooperatively
and justly. Over and above this they believed their religion dealt
with the other broad dimensions of man's existence, its mysteries, its
imponderables—how man and the universe came to be and why, the
place of mankind in the scheme of things, the nature of man and his
destiny, the meaning of pain and death, the meaning of life itself.
It also dealt with man's inner life, with guilt and forgiveness, with
doubt, faith, and hope. It dealt with man's need to work and play, to
worship and pray, his hunger for purpose and meaning, his desire to
love, to create, to discover his true identity, and to achieve self-
fulfillment.

The people of the shtetl early became aware of the fact that they
would be nearer to God if they reflected on these very things than if
they were concerned with political and economic activities. Yet they
were never permitted to forget that they must also be frightfully concerned with this world because there is where their children and their
children's children would have to live. The Lord would take care of
the business of the next world. Indeed, they were not as concerned
with the Four Horsemen of the Apocalypse as they were with the policeman, the soldier, the nobleman, and the priest.

Despite the rigidity of their religious system the worship of the shtetl
Jews did not degenerate into a mechanical experience. It was, for the
most of them, a vital, refreshing outpouring of adoration, reverence,
dreams, and hopes for self and for all mankind. Their prayers pre-
sented emotions more often than might be thought and they could reveal the drama of the universe in the minute, pouring out images and

similes, ideals and tones. It was as though the heart, mind, and soul were being laid open for God to see and to manipulate as He saw fit.

While it is true that the literature covering the whole area of Judaism is voluminous, throughout the years Jewish sages have made an effort to distill it so that it can be simply expressed and easily grasped, although it has and always will remain difficult to live by.

In the beginning God passed on to Moses 613 commandments which encompassed the spirit of Judaism. Later, David, in the fifteenth Psalm, reduced them to eleven: "Lord, who shall sojourn in thy Tabernacle? Who shall dwell upon Thy Holy mountain? He that walketh uprightly, and worketh righteousness, and speaketh truth in his heart; that hath no slander upon his tongue, nor doeth evil to his fellow, nor taketh up a reproach against his neighbor; in whose eyes a vile person is despised. But he honoreth them that fear the Lord; He that sweareth to his own hurt, and changeth not; He that putteth not out his money on interest, nor taketh a bribe against the innocent. He that doeth those things shall never be moved."

Then Isaiah reduced the spirit of Judaism to six elements (33:15); "He that walketh righteously, and speaketh uprightly; he that despiseth the gain of oppressions, that shaketh clear his hands from laying hold on bribes, that stoppeth his ears from hearing of blood, and shutteth his eyes from looking on evil."

And Micah reduced it to three elements: "It hath been told thee, O man, what is good, and what the Lord doth require of thee: only to do justly and to love mercy, and to walk humbly with thy God."

Then Isaiah once more reduced it to two elements (56:1): "Thus saith the Lord: Keep ye justice and do righteousness."

And finally Amos reduced the spirit of Judaism to one element (5:4): "Seek ye me, and ye shall live."

For these people, Jewishness was more than a set of beliefs and rituals, more than what was compressed into tenets and rules. Jewishness was not in the fruit but in the sap that stirred through the tissues of the tree. Jewishness was not only truth: it was vitality, joy; to some the only joy. The intellectual majesty of the Shema Yisroel, when translated into the language of their hearts, signified "it is a joy to be a Jew." And something else, the religion of these Jews included the thousands of threads which bound together a people scattered throughout the world.

"Seek ye me and ye shall live" was the master key which opened all doors for them, which gave them continuity and helped them remember the marvelous fact that life is indeed here with its tragic elements, but it is also here with its beauty, its grace, its love of God, in each child, and in all those who have a share in humanity. And, because this is so, man is able to prevail against the perils and hate of a sometimes cold and bitter world.

Oddly enough, the greatest peril that the people of the shtetl faced came from the "neighbors" who lived across the street from the shtetl and in whose mind the word "Jew" conjured up some kind of strange creature. Conspicuousness has ever been the great misfortune of Israel.

These neighbors were the people whom their Christ had specifically commanded: "Love thy neighbor as thyself." There is a story told which is appropriate at this point. A Jew was being chased through the street by a drunken Russian mob. He passed a church and ran into it. A service was in progress so he knelt with all the other members of the congregation. The priest noticed him and said quite loudly: "Will all the Jews in this church leave?" The Jew only hid deeper under the pew. Again the priest called out: "Will all Jews leave this church immediately!" At this, Jesus descended from the cross, walked to the Jew, took him by the arm and said: "Come, let us go. I don't think either one of us is wanted here."

Even if the Jews of two thousand years ago had a hand in the death of one of their own, the modern Christians have forgotten his last commandment: "Father, forgive them, for they know not what they do," as they go about the business of embarrassing, criticizing, punishing Jews of today.

Herein may lie, at least in part, the key to the problem of hatred— for those neighbors across the street from the shtetl did not love themselves, hence they could not love anyone else. They were impoverished, not only materially but spiritually; they constituted the host but they owned very little; they were ignorant; most of them were tillers of the soil; they had no artisans; few were tradesmen; and very, very few were professional men. They were taught to equate Judaism with heathenism; they suffered bitterly from Judophobia; most of them were graceless, loud, and blustering; a great majority of them suffered from a most deadly disease known as "debility." And the suffocating demands of the Czar and church hung over their heads until the Gordian knot was finally cut by the same sword which sliced through the Russian soul, leaving it still bleeding.

There was a strange paradox permeating the cultural atmosphere beyond the shtetl. On the one hand the Russian or Polish leaders, political, economic, and religious, did their best to follow the dictum of Nietzsche and his "will to power" philosophy, while on the other hand they read, with much interest and pride, the novels of Leo Tolstoy, who believed in an ethical system that included love and compassion.

The shtetl Jews thus found themselves in an analogous position. Believing the stereotype created in their minds, the Gentiles expected the Jews to behave in a certain way, which they refused to do. For this the Jews could not be forgiven, because it is a fact that men cannot forgive those whom they have injured. This basic element proved to be a vicious cycle which drove the two groups farther and farther apart. There was deep bitterness in the hearts of the shtetl people against their neighbors across the street, but seldom lasting hatred, for "vengeance is mine saith the Lord," and it is further written in Leviticus: "In righteousness shall you judge your neighbor."

The writer recalls well that, albeit he feared and distrusted those neighbors deeply, most of the time he felt pity and contempt for them rather than hatred. He was a member of a kingdom of priests— they were members of a kingdom of serfs; he could read and write— they were, by and large, ignorant; his concern in life was a deep sense of spiritual purpose—their main purpose in life was to grow up, have enough food to eat and vodka to drink. (Small wonder Jews from Eastern Europe developed such a passionate aversion toward alcoholism.) His greatest sense of superiority resulted from the contrast between his God and theirs. Their God was localized, specialized, and corporeal. He stayed in one place, He hung on the wall. He was made of wood, stone, and paper. (It is interesting to note that many non-Jews dislike Judaism because of its hostility toward images and art in general in relation to their religion.) Thus it was that the writer early developed a feeling of superiority in regard to his Gentile neighbors. (One suspects that here is, at least to a degree, another example of ethnocentrism.)

The people of the shtetl were well aware of God's concern for all mankind, even the enemies of the Jews. It is written in the Talmud that when the Egyptians were drowning in the Red Sea the angels in heaven were about to break out in songs of joy, but God silenced them with these words: "My creatures are perishing and ye are ready to sing."

Despite this outlook, there were times when the people of the shtetl had cause to wonder whether things could really be as dreadful as they seemed and to ponder the imponderable question: "If man is good, why does he do evil? If evil, why does he love good?" In regard to their Christian neighbors they simply reached the judgment that the love and wisdom which the Christian master displayed have been too frequently alloyed with bitterness, ignorance, and violence by his followers. They realized, furthermore, that they had to develop an antidote to the poison surrounding them, otherwise it could destroy them, because human values can be destroyed when people are persecuted for reasons over which they have no control and for which they are not responsible. So the people of the shtetl made a delicate adjustment to their environment and placed their lives under the watchful eye of self and of God, a mutual vigilance which kept alive the complicated pattern of personal and group survival.

To keep themselves from becoming impersonal, uncaring, faceless men and women and to achieve a measure of individuality, they turned more and more to the source of their strength and inspiration, the Book, for it was their books which helped them discover what is crucial to any culture—what is vital and lasting and what is superficial and leads to nowhere. It was in their books that they came

face to face with greatness. There will surely be many who will insist
that such behavior is another example of retreat; however, the shtetl
people would certainly have answered quietly and patiently that
truth cannot always be demonstrated with the aid of logic.

It was Mohammed who first called Jews the "People of the Book"
and with good reason, for they learned early in their history that
their strength lay less in their arms than in their minds, and if they
hoped to achieve the final harmony between God and man they had
better go about the business of learning more about both of them.
In their wandering they never possessed many "things" so they became preoccupied with the struggle of "ideas" rather than "things."
The Talmud sums up the shtetl philosophy about learning very well:
"The scholar takes precedence over the king." One is quite safe in
saying that in no other ethnic group has such a high value been placed
on the learned man as among Jews in general and among the people
of the shtetl in particular.

It was the apostate Disraeli who boasted with much acid as well
as accuracy, and with the pride that often survives apostasy, that his
ancestors were scholars at the time when the ancestors of his British
colleagues in the important body where he served were savages running wild somewhere in the bogs of England.

It is said in the Talmud: "He who teaches the traditions of his
fellow man is regarded as though he had formed and made him, and
brought him into the world, for it is written in Jeremiah [15:19],
'And if thou bring forth the precious out of the vile, thou shalt be
as My mouth.' " Thus the teacher in Israel believes that, as a result of his efforts, he gives the individual a second birth and a loftier
life. Maimonides, the great Jewish philosopher and teacher, in-
structed his followers clearly and emphatically that "every Jew is
obligated to study Torah whether he be poor or rich, in good health
or a sufferer, young or old. Even if he goes begging from door to door
and has a wife and children to support, he must set aside time for
study of the Torah. . . ." And how long must he continue to study?
Until his death. This applied particularly to the people of the shtetl.
If parents could not help the student in his studies then the neighbors

must. If the neighbors could not help the student in his studies then the community must, for the very good reason that the purpose of education was to prepare every person to fit into the kingdom of God which must be found in every community. Small wonder that the centuries spent in the shtetl may be considered one of the most creative episodes in the history of the Jews, for during that period they schooled themselves as no other group in their dedication to God and to His doctrine, out of which came their remarkable spiritual and intellectual outlook on life.

It was inevitable that the shtetl education would be religiously oriented. As inadequate and narrow as it was, it was education for a purpose. It was a specific preparation for the business of being a Jew, for serving God and the community, and for surviving a tough and mean environment. Men, women, and children of the shtetl, then, were imbued with a rare dedication to learning.[7] There was very little of the attitude that may be found in so many areas of the world, referred to as "anti-intellectualism." There was little emphasis, thus, on report cards or ratings. There were few drop-outs there. To be sure, education was often dull and always difficult, but it was often exciting and dramatic. The young people learned early in life that they would have to struggle with the world around them and come to terms with it and the only way to do this successfully was to be prepared with the proper tools—in their case, knowledge and wisdom. And then there was Rabbi Judah ibn Tibbon, a great sage of the olden days, always standing over their shoulders saying to each one personally: "My son, make your books companions. Let your shelves be your treasure grounds and gardens. If you are weary, change from garden to garden. Your desire will renew itself and your soul will be filled with delight."

As has been noted, in the shtetl there was little of the business of

[7] The writer's father, who was himself a refugee from Czarist Russia, who was unlettered, and who spoke English very poorly (albeit with much charm and wit), often admitted that one of his supreme thrills in life was living long enough to see his children well educated. He did live long enough to send all his children to college and to be present when one son received an M.D. and another a Ph.D.

social status—learning was the basic element which gave one any status at all. Most of the people were learned enough in Torah so that they did not have to look up to the others, and those who were highly learned in Torah were wise enough not to look down at the rest. They fervently believed, furthermore, that when two people exchange ideas with each other they each have two ideas. So they continued to study all their lives, for they had discovered an old truism: if one stops studying today he becomes ignorant tomorrow.

The writer recalls vividly his own experience at the *cheder* (Hebrew school) in the shtetl. He remembers to this day the *melamed* (teacher), a little old man with a white beard who smelled of stale clothes and food. He was not really very worldly, but the children considered him a *Tzaddik* (wise and good man); he enjoyed great prestige and his word was law.[8] He seemed to possess a diabolical determination to instruct his few scatterbrained pupils in Hebrew, in prayer, in the Torah, and the Talmud. Our melamed made it clear in no uncertain terms that piety was not as important as study, that it was not only with our lips but with our lives that vital Jewish faith became the richest and most valid perspective for living in our topsy-turvy world. Indeed, that little, old, dried-up, impoverished *rebbi* made us understand well that, whereas it may not take much of a man to be a Jew, it does take all there is of him.

There were about ten pupils in that class, poorly dressed, always hungry, with *piisen* (sideburns) just beginning to show and well protected from evil by the *tzitzes* we wore under our shirts.[9] We spent the long day in the cheder around a worn-out, unclean table. The Torah was our Homer, our Virgil, our theology, as well as our geography, our history, and our civics.

Oddly enough, the writer recalls something else which excited him in the business of studying Torah and which is best left to Freud

---

[8] He believed without question in the talmudic dictum which says: "Do not receive a pupil under the age of six years, but after that stuff him like an ox."

[9] *Tzitzes* are ritual fringes worn as a visible reminder to fulfill the 613 precepts of the Torah (Num. 15:37–39).

to explain. He recalls that there was an inexplicable sensuality found in the pages of the Torah smelling slightly of the barnyard. But by far the most dramatic and the most inspiring aspect of studying the Torah was the idea that tomorrow in the Torah we would find new adventures—even new frontiers. Tomorrow would be another chapter and a new beginning. Studying the Torah held an ever-recurring promise: it was a kind of work and every bit as serious as play, which would open the magic of the universe before us even though for only a fleeting moment, and all for what purpose? So that these scrawny, little, runny-nosed, frightened dreamers of the shtetl could someday help change the world. So we sat patiently on the hard benches and studied the material collected by sages and saints who got it from the one truly reliable source of information, from God Himself.

Because of the political and economic restrictions imposed upon the Jews of the shtetl, their opportunities for earning a livelihood were limited. A student of economics with a keen sense of humor and a knowledge of Yiddish would classify the people of the shtetl as "luft-menschen," literally, people who earn their living from the air, but actually by their wits. They were forbidden to own land, to join guilds; only commerce was open to them. To be sure, in large centers Jews often got into the banking business, which amounted merely to the sinful business of lending money—*usury* it was called when the Jews did it. However, in the shtetl there was little opportunity for this sort of banking. There most people were quite poor, but even the most impoverished were not paupers in the ordinary sense—that is to say, beggars, tramps, or plain failures. There was another name for a Jew who was very poor: he was a *Kasrilik*.[10] A kasrilik, one must understand, is indeed a poor man but one who has not allowed poverty to degrade him. He laughs at it, he is cheerful about it, and in some ways he is a little proud of it. To him riches could be not only unsatisfactory but could even be a curse. Indeed, in the shtetl one might deliberately choose poverty for himself and his family in

[10] Sholom Aleichem, *The Old Country* (New York: Crown Publishing Co., 1946), 1. Kasrilevka is the name of the shtetl about which Aleichem writes so perceptively—hence the name "Kasrilik."

order to study the Torah, fulfill its commitments, and thus benefit from God's promises.

In general, money did not play a very important role in the lives of the shtetl Jews. They went through life making some sort of living, and there was no temptation to speculate in financial matters. Their only speculation had to do with social changes around them, with the next steps taken by the Czar, or by Rasputin, or the local leaders, and how these would affect their lives. Most Jews lived in similar houses, slept in similar beds, ate about the same food and had about the same income. Socially they were about as democratic as it is humanly possible to be. To be sure, the scholar, the student of the Torah, ranked a little higher in the scale of social stratification, or perhaps the cattle buyer made a little more money. Some of them even had help, but few had servants. The few social distinctions were not based on income. Indeed, there was little temptation in the shtetl to keep up with the Cohens.

Tolstoy once concluded that "personal misery is the result not of man's need but of his abundance." Whereas it is true that in the matter of natural resources, the people of the shtetl were poor and had trouble keeping the body alive, in the matter of keeping the soul alive they lived in abundance. As a matter of fact, along the long road the Jews have traveled, when they became too involved in their own dialectics, when the wall of law which they built around them became a prison rather than a sanctuary, when their glorious Torah was no longer a thing to live by but to live for, all they had to do in order to clear up their vision was to turn to their holidays, their stories, and their humor. Suddenly they were able not only to preserve but even to enlarge their outlook, their dignity, and their moral powers, no matter what was going on around them.

Somewhere in one's faith there must be a growing edge if it is to keep pace with and be able to interpret and evaluate one's experience. In the case of the shtetl Jews this growing edge was to be found in their holiday rituals. Centuries ago sacred characteristics were assigned to the Jewish holidays—they were created to be festivals of

hope. To be sure, all times are God's seasons, but the seasons of the
Jewish holidays were special seasons for they had a special siren
voice which summoned man to slip away from the ordinary world
around him, from the world of iniquities and tears, from the world
of sweat and ugliness. The soul needs mystery for its substance, and
it was during the seasons of the holidays that the souls of the shtetl
people received such spiritual nourishment. Every holiday became
a sort of iron lung in which they could, for a time, breathe freely
and easily.

Those were the days when they became equal to the whole world.
Surrounded by ugliness and hate, they found inspiration and beauty
in the rituals with which they surrounded the most ordinary aspects
of every one of their holidays. During these special periods their dark
present disappeared, and their minds were filled with visions of their
glorious past and their hope for the faith in a better future. During
other days the people of the shtetl could see the "watch," but on the
holidays they could see the "watchmaker"; on ordinary days they repeated the twenty-third Psalm, but on those days they knew the
Shepherd. Those were the days when the people of the shtetl knew
that their "times were in His hands."

It must be well understood that to those people holiness in Judaism
did not imply a removal from life but rather an immersion in it, and
the holidays were so constructed that Jews could truly become deeply
immersed in the unfathomable that belongs to God and not to man—
the unfathomable that man can approach only through his intense
feelings.

All the holidays did much to sustain and strengthen the people of
the shtetl. They reminded them of the fields and vineyards of their
ancestors in Palestine; they brought a sense of freedom and higher
purpose into their lives; they gave them dignity and purpose and filled
their hearts with renewed hope, beauty, and inspiration. However,
the Sabbath was the most sanctified and blessed of all holidays—it is
the covenant between God and the children of Israel forever, for it
is written "blessed be the Sabbath, the queen of days, which brings

unto Israel enrichment of soul . . . even as Israel has kept the Sabbath, so the Sabbath has kept Israel."[11]

The Sabbath in the shtetl was like a monastic seclusion for one day, designed to bring peace and harmony. Nothing could enter it— the wall around it was impenetrable. It was a day to visit with God, face to face. On that day every man, woman, and child became something unique, a distinct personality, significant, important, standing tall, with a shadow longer than ever. On that day something happened to their souls which broke away from the cramped, dismal, everyday life and soared high among the heavenly bodies; on that day they did not feel their shortcomings, their bonds, their narrowness, because on that day they could stand before God and repeat the ancient prayer with deep feeling; "My God, the soul which Thou has given me is pure. Thou didst create it, Thou didst breathe it into me." On that day the morning stars sang together and all the sons of God shouted for joy. On that day they tasted eternal life even if it was for only a brief moment.

If, by some chance, life became too unbearable for the shtetl Jews, if there were moments when even their religion failed to impose dignity and give strength for daily living, they were driven back on their sense of humor to be found in their Yiddish stories. It has been wisely said that humor is not what you create but with which you create. This was particularly true in Jewish life.

It was La Rochefoucauld who once keenly observed: "The world is a tragedy to those who feel and a comedy to those who think." The people of the shtetl were a fine example of a group who, by the very nature of things, were forced to feel and to think. They felt to a rare degree the pathos and absurdities, follies and pride, strength and weaknesses of their own lives and of all mankind. To them, humor itself was a version of sadness, and their stories demonstrated

---

[11] To this day, during the Friday evening services in the Reform temples the congregation is reminded that "they who keep the Sabbath and call it a delight, rejoice in Thy Kingdom. All who hallow the seventh day shall be gladdened by Thy goodness. This day is Israel's festival of the spirit, sanctified and blessed by Thee, the most precious of days, a symbol of the joy of creation."

deep sympathy and feeling, well mixed with irony. In short their humor and delight in life was a mixture of the fundamentals of life: piety and passion, food and drink, birth, death and after-life, and their eternal confrontation with the Almighty Himself; indeed, those shtetl people had the tall gift of fun and laughter.

To be sure, religious literature one studied seriously, profoundly, respectfully, but the Yiddish story one took to his heart. The Yiddish story is essentially a story of the unimportant little man. There are many variations of this little man: he is a fool or a wise man, he is a scholar or a *balebos* (business man), he is a butcher or a melamed, he is a *schlemiele* or a saint, but whoever he is, he bears the burden of his Jewish spirit with pride and joy; he is long-suffering but persistent, lovingly ironical but compassionate, with a whimsical twinkle in his eye and a satirical twist in his view of the universe. The Yiddish story seems to possess those strange and dramatic qualities which appeal to one's imagination and challenge his ingenuity; and, indeed, it convinces one that perhaps many people can conquer the world, but only a Tevye or a Moishe or a Schloime can learn to face up to it and to live in it.

As important as the content of the Yiddish story is the fact that it was written in a very unusual language. Israel Zangwill once said that the Yiddish language incorporates the essence of a life which is distinctive and unlike any other. Despite this, there is probably no other language anywhere on which so much criticism has been heaped. Be that as it may, here is an observation beyond dispute: good Yiddish contains a trinity of virtues—an expression of deep feeling for the suffering in life, a profound suggestion of humor, and a discriminating sense of the rhythm of the spoken word, plus the fact that through the medium of this language much more may be implied than actually said. This remains certain: the voice of the Yiddish lent itself well to the telling of the shtetl stories.

In regard to the humor as well as the pathos of the shtetl story, it is enough to say that in the lives of the millions of Jews of Eastern Europe, the gaiety and laughter, the tears and mourning, the humor and satire of the Yiddish tale proved a great therapy. Neither persecution nor poverty could destroy their life force which was nourished so bountifully by the delightful and refreshing tales of intimate Jewish life in the shtetl.

If we cannot penetrate the imponderable recesses of the shtetl mind, we can know this: here was a minority group forced to think in order to survive and as a result they were able to condition themselves to such a fashion that they could gratify most of their vital needs within the framework of the complexity of their particular type of life. How narrow and stilted was their prison they never realized and, despite the fact that they lived in a pluriverse, their life was not a fragmented, a paralleled thing of shreds and patches with its secular and sacred compartments. With them Judaism permeated the whole life of every man, woman, and child. They were able to cut through the distortions of centuries with the same ease as they drew their glasses of tea from the samovar and to recreate the texture of the great Hebraic minds with the same enthusiasm as they consumed their "gefilte" fish, as they did their best to relive the remarkable adventures of their forefathers from whom they drew their passion for eternity.

Along the way the people of the shtetl learned well that if the rubbish surrounding most of life is cleared away, it becomes clear that what ultimately happens to an individual or a group will depend largely on the faiths that move them. In the final analysis, men live by what they love and hope for, and they can endure and be strong only if life has an ongoing, consummating meaning and purpose. Thus it was that simple, everyday situations in their lives became invested with great significance.

Out of the awareness and acceptance of the uniqueness of their religion the people of the shtetl reached several conclusions. They had to remain Jews because there was no other religion for which they could change it—every other religion had something they could not accept. As they understood religion, Judaism offered them a life lived as fully and richly and meaningfully as possible in each passing hour of existence. Then there was that covenant made with God which they could not break now or ever. (Exod. 19:5). Thus is was that they continued to practice what has been called by sophisticated theorists an "eccentric, fossilized" form of religion, and no matter what they were doing—baking bread, mending shoes, chopping wood, selling grain, or reading Torah—their souls were ever on their knees.

In the shtetl, people were protected by traditions. Their religion invested their existence as Jews with intimations of immortality. Knowing the culture of their forefathers they felt that it enriched and stimulated them. The prophets, sages, and teachers of the Jewish past were their companions, and no matter what the "neighbor" across the street might say or do, they knew that Judaism and Jewishness were honorable, meaningful realities and that knowledge armored their sense of worth.[12] Indeed, they needed that armor desperately for when they gazed across the street they heard the word *zid* spit at them. There across the way was ever the stink of garbage, vodka, and unwashed bodies, everywhere the blight of ignorance, superstition, and ugliness. In truth, the horror was always there, just across the street, just around the corner day and night—it was always there no matter what was going on in the shtetl—a birth or a death, a wedding, or a funeral.

Despite what they saw and heard across the street, in general, the people of the shtetl did not altogether agree with Hobbes, the great social philosopher, who said of man: "His life is nasty, brutal and short"; nor would they accept the Calvinistic doctrine that "human nature is not fit to be trusted nor men never good but through necessity." They argued that since all men were made in the image of God, they were, by nature, good; thus every life has sanctity, whether fulfilled or unfulfilled. Their outlook on life, despite their great difficulties, was simple: "Whoever walks in the ways of the Lord is wise for he is doing right"; and they continued to do their best to walk in the ways of the Lord. There was no one to speak for the shtetl Jews—there was no one priest, no one prophet—each one was a priest and each one was a prophet.

To be sure, there were pathetic apostates and despicable informers,

<hr />

[12] Milton Steinberg, *A Partisan Guide to the Jewish Problem* (New York: Bobbs-Merrill Co., 1945), 119.

but these individuals were viewed as having fallen by the wayside, as people who had somehow lost God and found evil, which left them with no reverence for life and no respect for the sacredness of human well-being. But, then, even these must be pitied, for in a sense, God Himself is responsible for their actions. For did He not say: "I form the light and create darkness: I make peace, and create evil: . . ." (Isaiah 45:7)

Despite the narrowness of their lives, the people of the shtetl had a surprisingly wholesome outlook on life with its seeming contradictions. They did not assume, as a matter of course, that men's acts will improve merely if they accept the assumption of God, the soul and immortality, and the concept of heaven and hell. The Talmud told them the passions are not all evil, for if it were not for them no one would marry a wife, beget children, build a house, or do any work. As a matter of fact, they were not overly concerned with the concept of sin—either original or acquired. They believed that one cannot any more talk himself out of his sins than he can talk himself into them. Both require action. They felt that doing the right things now as best one can is far more important than merely "believing" in something, for it has been written that one hour of good deeds on this earth is worth more than the whole life of the world to come.

Judaism in the shtetl was first a dedication to God and second a dedication to a system of laws. The Jews of that community believed that they did not sin against these laws but against people; that they did not break laws but rather that laws broke them. In short, the goal of their past, present, and future was the fulfillment of God's testament year by year, day by day, and hour by hour.

So these strange, stubborn, dedicated anachronisms of history stood before each other, told their stories and argued about the Talmud, stood before their "neighbors" across the street and bargained with them and pitied them, and stood before their Maker and poured out their hearts in fervent prayer. And finally they stood before their families, where first they learned the meaning of the sound of the Shofar, clear and untouched, beyond the measure of time and space.

VI

By Wisdom a House Is Built

$\mathcal{T}$ he shtetl Jews would have respectfully disagreed with those social scientists who insist that the family is not universal (the anthropologists give as examples the Kibbutz community in Israel and the Nazar community of southern India). To be sure, the scientists do add that the problem depends on how one defines the family.[1] And speaking of definitions, the shtetl Jews would have taken issue with all social scientists who define Judaism simply as a religion like all other religions—a concept which has nothing to do with race or politics. This, they would have insisted, is both hypocritical and self-contradictory. They could define Judaism, all right. It was to them not only a system of beliefs but one which was nationally and racially self-segregating, and also one which automatically created its own culture and its own ethnic ghettos.[2] A little more refined, their definition of a Jew was simple and to the point: Any person who follows the teachings of the Torah is a Jew; if not, he is a Gentile. As for the Kibbutz community in Israel in which children are reared away from their families and in which traditional religious services

[1] William N. Stephens, *The Family in Cross-Cultural Perspective* (New York: Holt, Rinehart and Winston, Inc., 1963), 2, 3.

[2] Arthur Koestler, *The Trail of the Dinosaur and Other Essays* (New York: Macmillan Co., 1955), 108.

have been eliminated, the shtetl people would have said that such practices would destroy the Jews faster than any pogrom ever could.

The Jews of the shtetl community did not have access to any ethnographic material whatsoever, so they had no problem defining the family and, in the light of their long history, their particular experience, and their deep awareness of the truths surrounding life they were convinced that the family must be a universal phenomenon. To them the family was first in the social reality of human beings not only because it was so ordained by their God but because the cycle of life begins and ends under conditions of dependency—not mere physical and economic dependency but, even more vitally important, psychic dependency. Where could this dependency be more ideally faced than in the family? The shtetl Jews would have answered that wherever we find human beings we find the family. To them the family was the source of all specifically human behavior and, in the case of the Jews, the source of all specifically Jewish behavior. In the shtetl the family was the agency which gave special markings to its members, not mere skin markings, but those etched deeply into the mind, the heart, the spirit, and the subconscious. It was the Jewish home in that unique community where values were handed down from generation to generation, nurtured in cells of peace, inspiration, strength, and divine direction, giving the young a feeling of harmony with the past, helping them generate a dream of the future, and acting as their unfailing source of spiritual rejuvenation.

Reverence for the home has long been one of the most fruitful and most rewarding of Jewish ideals. In the shtetl it filled the impoverished homes with an indescribable charm, it covered family life with a genuine sanctity, it wove into a strong fabric the words of God, the legends of the past, the sayings of the sages, the preachments of the prophets, and the songs of the poets. Indeed, it transformed the home into more than a castle, it transformed it into a sanctuary. Its table became an altar, its meal a solemn sacrifice, and the father a ministering priest. And to protect its members from the baseness and ugliness of the outside world, the home was further guarded by the prayers inscribed "on the doorposts of the house and upon the gates."

All in all, the atmosphere of that home tended to turn the hearts of the parents to the children and the hearts of the children to the parents, binding the members of the group to each other in a strong and lasting bond.

No matter what the shtetl Jew thought about his place in the world at large, in his home he had to admit that he did not belong only to himself. And because the Jews of the shtetl refused to compromise their convictions about the value of the family, the words of the prophets are still influencing the lives of half the people on earth.

It was said long ago that it is not good that man should be alone, for the Talmud does not regard the individual man as a self-sufficient personality. He is complete through matrimony. "The unmarried person lives without joy, without blessing, and without good." Rabbi Eliezer, the sage, had some very definite attitudes about those who live alone, whether they "like it or not." He said: "An unmarried man is not a complete man, and a woman is an unfinished vessel until she marries; and he who has no wife misses everything and has no joy and no bliss." In short, an unmarried person is not a whole person in the full sense of the term.

There is also another good reason for having a family. The Messiah cannot come until all the souls created by God have been fitted to the earthly bodies destined for their reception on earth. Thus it is necessary to marry and produce children who might in turn reproduce the longed-for Redeemer.

As far back as the Jewish group-memory goes, human life has been an experience in creation, and to the shtetl Jews the family is the best expression of all creativeness.[3] This is one of the basic reasons why their families have survived in spite of unrelenting persecution.

[3] The writer's mother taught him, not in so many specific terms but rather with attitudes, values, simple bits of philosophy, that there are, in the final analysis, three truly important, worthwhile, and lasting creative opportunities with which man is blessed: to plant a tree, to write a book, and to bear a child. To make barren earth flourish, to put down on paper ideas, thoughts and dreams, and to create a new life is to share in God's divine plan. And while there is much of the selfish motive involved in all three actions, yet ultimately they all three remain for posterity.

Jews have long insisted that man's progress through the ages has been rooted in the power of thought (the thought that can and will take shape in action), and the ideal vehicle for shaping and expediting that action must be the family. The shtetl family believed that every child became the epitome, as it were, of the history of his own family. Furthermore, they believed that in order to understand a people, a nation, or a society one must first understand the nature of their families. This was particularly true in the case of the shtetl, where most of the facets of life revolved around the family circle. So there was no question in their minds that, despite the dynamic social changes which might take place in the world of man, the family would remain.

It is indeed paradoxical that in the narrow, ugly, miserable streets of the shtetl there developed a rare and beautiful family life which has been far more important in Jewish life than many of the outer events and struggles recorded by historians, theologians, and ethnologists.

In the shtetl the purpose of the family was basically two-fold, to perpetuate the "race" and to bring happiness, strength, and security to its members. The home was the secret joy of the shtetl. Outside the windows there may be the ghostly shadow of the hydraheaded monster, persecution; outside the walls, the cold and the rain; under the floor, the damp, grey, hated soil of the alien land; but inside was ever the presence of the prophet Elijah, Eliyahu Ha-Nair, the most popular and most romantic of all Jewish prophets—the prophet who protects the poor, cares for the righteous, watches over those who are in danger and who despair, and, most important of all, who will announce the coming of the Messiah.

"By wisdom was that home built and by understanding was it established." Indeed, in that home were men and women, fathers and mothers, offspring, grandparents, grandchildren, and siblings; there were tears and laughter; there was tenderness and pathos, courage and cowardice, humility and arrogance, serenity and discipline, and the sheer, simple beauty and magic which came from genuine love and family devotion. All this was blessed by the spirit of holiness which turned the home into a sanctuary, for "except the Lord build the house, they labor in vain who build it: unless the Lord keep the city, the watchman but waketh in vain. It is in vain for you to rise up early, sit up late, to eat the bread of sorrows: for so he giveth his beloved sleep" (Psalms 127:1, 2). Thus it was that from the Jewish home emanated a certain mysterious air which the non-Jew could not comprehend. Small wonder he was suspicious about what went on there.

The inner solidarity of the shtetl was actually the result of strong family ties. In this familial sanctum deep bonds of sympathy were woven between members in many ways: rituals, holidays, commemoration of special events, joyous and sad. Here each member had dignity and status; here each was an intimate part of a long and beautiful tradition. Furthermore, the outward manifestation of separation tended to intensify the self-consciousness of the family so that the members built up a unit most unique among men.

From a sociological point of view the shtetl was a family-centered community. The family there was strong and cohesive, held together by deep religious feelings, by traditional ties of loyalty, by a common need for protection, by mutual dependence, and, finally, by the absence of any other group to which the individual in that social atmosphere could belong. Without the family he would stand alone, insecure, unprotected, and isolated.[4]

In those days religion was mingled with every action of family life. It was natural that the men in the home would envelop themselves every morning in white shawls with black stripes and wind bands of leather about their foreheads and left arms while murmuring words which were realistic and meaningful day after day. It was normal for all to participate in the blessings before meals and drink and, on Friday evening, to see the mother of the home extending her hands

---

[4] Sociologists recognize that group solidarity is largely dependent upon the frequency, motivation, and emotional quality of the interaction of its members. Common goals, social contracts, mutual accountability result in the degree of morale, loyalty, enthusiasm, and lasting power of a group. Paul B. Norton and Chester L. Hunt, *Sociology* (New York: McGraw-Hill Book Co., 1964).

over the candlelights in prayer. It was commonplace for all members of the family to take part in many of the holiday rituals which took place in the home. With those people no institution, not even the shul, could supplant the home in the teachings of Judaism. They believed that the family is and must be the central agency for teaching religion to the child, for God Himself once said: "I know him (Avrom) that he will command his children and his household after him and they shall keep the way of the Lord." Thus it was in the shtetl that marriage and family living became a spiritual as well as an ethical, social, biological, and economic business. Next to the business with God, the Jews of the shtetl considered no "business" as important as family business for it was the machinery which repaired the social fabric of their group, closed its ranks, dramatized Jewish life in such a way as to bolster the waverers who might be seduced into following after false gods.

As the more dominant partner in the home, the husband was admonished to treat his wife with tenderness and understanding, for it is written "whoever loves his wife as himself and honors her more than himself, he shall know peace." The key element in the relationship between husband and wife in the shtetl family was respect, and fidelity was expected from the husband as well as the wife; he was to love her, to honor her, and be true to her. There was, to be sure, a patriarchal emphasis in the shtetl family organization, particularly in regard to the principle of superiority of the male—the husband superior to the wife, brothers superior to sisters. "Blessed be God that He did not make me a woman." So goes the Hebrew prayer, typical of man's effort to make of her the weaker sex.

The shtetl wife, in her simple way, realized why he was "protesting too much," and offered her version of the above prayer: "Blessed be the Lord who created according to His will," and went about the business of being a woman, a wife, a mother, a member of the community all at one time.

Actually there was no role conflict in the shtetl family. Their culture solved this problem. The husband believed that he was the authority in the family, but the wife knew she was—this was the secret of their successful marriage and family relationship (the secret of any successful marriage and family relationship, then and now, there or here).

The Talmud seems to sum up the relationship this way: "God dwells in a pure and loving home. . . . In a home where the wife is a daughter of a God-fearing man, the husband has God for a father-in-law. Not money but character is the best dowry of a wife. . . . Who is rich? He whose wife's actions are comely. . . . Who is happy? He whose wife is modest and gentle. . . . When his wife dies, a man's world is darkened, his step is slow, his mind is heavy; she dies in him, he in her. . . . A man must not make a woman weep, for God counts her tears. . . . Marriages are made in heaven. . . . A man's happiness is all of his wife's creation. . . ."

If the father was the head of the shtetl family, the mother was the heart. All mothers are a "species" unto themselves, for the simple reason that they play the key role in the whole business of conceiving, developing, giving birth to and molding the child, which is the *raison d'etre* of the life process, the basis of family life in particular and social life in general, for it is written that "he who leaves children is never considered as dead."

The shtetl mother played this role well but she possessed some exceptional qualities over and above this natural role. The unique history of Judaism, the style of living developed by the Jews over the centuries, the purpose of the Jewish family, particularly in the shtetl, gave the Jewish mother in that community characteristics possessed by mothers in few other groups and in few other areas. She had a deep belief in God, a dream of a decent future, and an unbreakable faith in her family, especially in her children whom she did her best to overfeed, overclothe, overprotect, and lovingly overspoil. Behind God himself, behind the Torah, behind the plaintive cries of the Psalmist and the disturbing words of the prophets were the needs, hopes, dreams of her family.

Despite her limited horizon and her preoccupation with seemingly petty affairs, there were always surprising wonders in her world, concealed from most eyes, yet she could sometimes get a rare view of them, as if a curtain were raised which permitted her an unusual sight of scenes ordinarily hidden. There must have been moments when she did not believe such scenes were possible except that there they were. There was too much to commit to memory, so that each time she saw the scene it was a new experience for her—it was there for any one who could lift his eyes to it. Indeed, to her, Jewish life was not inspired by thundering sermons nor by impressive demonstrations, but by the simple words of Ruth speaking to Naomi, by the wisdom of Solomon, by the songs of David's harp singing across the ages, and by the quiet and almost invisible hand guided by the Almighty Himself.

Yet all her life the shtetl mother found herself struggling against three major elements. The first struggle was against the danger that she might not have the endurance, the wisdom, the time, the resolution, and the heroism to interpret the world and all of its devices in terms of Judaism, for the Psalmist (86:11, 12) had made her purpose clear long ago when he asked God Himself "Teach me Thy way, O Lord; I will walk in thy truth: unite my heart to fear thy name. I will praise thee, O Lord my God, with my whole heart: and I will glorify Thy name for evermore."

The second struggle was against dirt, hunger, and poverty. To the typical shtetl mother God was, along with many other things, a God of clean plates and tasty meals, and her prayers were ever that she be a *behrya*, a good housekeeper. She would consume the world in a thousand fires of cooking and baking so that her husband and children would not go hungry.

The third struggle was against the fear that her children would marry out of the faith. She would work her fingers to the bone, she would go hungry, she would do without clothes, she would bargain with the Lord or even the devil on any bases they wished just so her children would marry within Judaism.

Although she was well aware of the fact that she did not enjoy the position in marriage which her husband did—her education was poor, she was deprived of many communal privileges, she could not go out to work, she did not have his authority in familial matters—actually in many ways she had an unwritten authority and an importance which he did not have. There were other positive factors in her favor—she was exempt from particular duties during certain periods of the month, she had the beautiful and inspiring privilege of lighting the Sabbath candles, she had the difficult but rewarding job of running the household, and finally, she had the status given to her by God Himself. She sensed from childhood that God had somehow given her a very special job in His scheme of things—to mold and shape her children according to His will—and thus the success or failure of God's plan for the Jews rested on her individual shoulders, and with such heavy responsibilities. Her argument was simply that if the shul may be likened to the Jewish mind in the Jew's relationship to God, then her family may be likened to his spinal cord. And to generate the vital force which impelled her to fulfill this awesome function in the lifestream of her people, she turned to the Psalmist with the prayer, "God is our refuge and strength, a very present help in trouble" (46:1), and to the words the Lord had spoken to her people long ago: "I will never fail you nor forsake you. Be strong and brave. Only observe all the laws which I handed down to you, turn neither to the right nor to the left, that you may prosper wherever you go." Thus she was sustained by a spiritual strength of which God was at once symbol and essence, evocator and voice.

Her outlook on life was simple, steadfast, irrevocable, and sweetly stubborn. She did not disguise her feelings, and she did not run away. She realized that she was not very wise, but she also realized that she was sure of things, very sure.

She recognized well the fact that in the singularly cheerless world surrounding the shtetl a human spirit less insulated would break in a short time. She was proud of her Hebraic heritage and of the part she played in continuing that image.

She had the deeply rooted and firmly established habit of thinking that God had chosen her family among all families in the world and was personally watching over its members and would assure their destiny. To be sure, in a material sense, there was little to be gained from being God's chosen people. In this respect all it had brought

them had been pain, suffering, and rejection; however, in matters of
the spirit, there was something else, for it had brought them spiritual
dignity comparable to few others, a pride and an independence, a
strength and a dream, a purpose and a vision without which her
people would have perished and returned to the dust from which they
came. Suppose the rest of the world did not agree with her, suppose
they said she, her family, and her outlook were all wrong, she would
have answered by rolling up her sleeves, putting on her apron and
going into the kitchen to make chicken noodle soup. Indeed, just as
Jacob wrestled with the angel and won, so are the world's victories
won, large or small. To her way of thinking this ideal was not the
product of a whim or a passing fancy—her forefathers had shed blood
and suffered untold hardship to prove it.

Once this point was settled in her mind, everything else was settled, and she could go about the business of expediting God's will.
And God's will meant that she was, in large measure, responsible
for making the Jewish family, binding it together, perpetuating its
traditions and customs, teaching the children to carry on the cycle,
and bringing peace, comfort, and warmth into the home.

Indeed, the shtetl wife and mother was an unforgettable creature,
truly an important part in the jigsaw of creation. She was warm and
responsive, she was never an onlooker in life, she was always in the
middle of it—things happened to her and she happened to them. She
showed the members of her family how to suffer and how to be happy,
how to cry and how to laugh, how to love and how to accept the inevitable in life. She could be gentle and she could be rough. She
knew that she was desperately needed by her husband and children
alike. She had a good imagination too. All around her she saw miracles—in the birth of her children, in the health of her husband, in
the warmth of her fireside, in the rising bread and her boiled potatoes,
in the promise of the Friday night candles and in the calmness of the
Sabbath peace. She lived her days in complete astonishment as she
moved around her house which sometimes seemed to her to be beyond the conditions of time and space.

And when her work was finished, the shtetl wife and mother took time out on the Sabbath afternoon to read the *Teitsch-chumash*, the Yiddish paraphrase of the Torah. "Be thou a blessing," the Lord had said to her and she tried to be.[5]

No matter her devotion to God, her love of family, her dedication to Judaism, her abiding need to be useful, and her subordination of personal aims and energies in the business of having and rearing a family, there were times when it was difficult to "be a blessing." Somewhere in her being were deep hurts and fears which did not go away easily. To be sure, her love needs were satisfied through her attachment to her husband and children, and her status and role were clear in the social structure of the shtetl, so that she had no uncertain attitudes about her function in life and very few unreal fears and unrealistic expectations. She was certain of what she wanted out of life and, in most instances, she was also certain how she could achieve her goals.

Among Jews the feeling about home has ever been that wherever the mother is, there is the home. The mother had no illusions about her importance in the family circle despite the traditional and time-honored view regarding the superiority of her husband. In the final analysis it was she who was the assertive, the lively, the demanding one, the manager, counselor, and confidante.

It is interesting to note that to her way of thinking even the "future" life was, in a sense, a mixed blessing. To be sure, she looked forward to heaven as a place where clothes did not get dirty, where food did not have to be cooked and dishes did not have to be washed,

---

[5] A good example of such an unforgettable person was the author's mother. After a half century the writer still marvels at her unbelievable and breathtaking courage and strength. She reared her children alone for many years in that lonely, frightening shtetl set against the haunted twilight sky, and she literally stole them out of Russia not once but twice. Undramatically and quietly she calmly sacrificed herself in order that they might have a peaceful and a decent future. Yet throughout the years she remained warm and sympathetic, determined and sensitive. Into her life, filled with conflict between painful reality and vivid imagination, came understanding and illumined truth, insight, and a rare capacity for weighing human needs. One of her finest qualities was her concern over honor. To her, honor was a supreme value, for to her it was, in the words of Romain Gary, "an affirmation of dignity, a declaration of man's superiority to all that befalls him." Indeed, it was her conviction that if people are to have dignity there must be tragic experience.

and children did not have to be cared for, yet in her heart, she did not really approve of such an existence. She would be out of place there. She was certain that she would have to find something worthwhile to do in heaven—things to straighten up, corners to sweep, wings to mend, celestial goodies to prepare, like making golden chicken noodle soup—and God Himself might be given a few suggestions on how to run the world more efficiently and more peacefully.

But the shtetl wife and mother had little time for this dreaming and little energy for the black despair of agonizing of the soul. She had to observe the world and to reflect on her observations with directness and dispatch. She had to get back to the business of scrimping and saving and making her family feel loved.

Yet there were things that gnawed at her and brought her sleepless nights and prompted her to say an extra prayer or two. Her overall concern was ever with the individual "life's crises" in her family group in which she played so important a role and for which she must be prepared at all times: birth, puberty, marriage, and death. These and other crises in her family's journey through life called for hard work, careful planning, much self-discipline and a great deal of spiritual strength. Of this last she had an abundance, for hers was not a maybe religion.

And always there was the enemy across the street with his insults, his threat of physical pain, and his hatred for her family and for what they stood.[6] As she looked across the street to that other neighborhood and heard, felt, and saw it filled high with hatred and bigotry, thundering at her from all sides, the best she could do was to exclaim with the Psalmist: "O Lord, how long shall the wicked exult?" For the answer she turned to Hosea (6:1, 2): "Come, and let us return unto the Lord: for He hath torn, and He will heal us; He hath smitten, and He will bind us up." Just the same, in some manner or other, quietly, slowly, she must play her small part in fighting tyranny. In-

---

[6] There was, of course, the ever-present danger of a pogrom bursting like a flame into the shtetl. The word "pogrom" in Russian literally means "destruction without pity." The writer, even as a child, sensed its imminence many times, and it is a feeling which is unforgettable.

deed, this she knew without putting it into words: a learned man, trained by mental discipline and culture and deeply imbued with Judaism, is the strongest bulwark against tyranny. Give her son a book and she would put him up against any soldier, any zealot, any bigot, and in the end he would prove victorious.

Her answer to the poverty and economic stagnation which haunted most people in the shtetl was a secret mechanism especially planted in Jewish wives and mothers by God Himself. In the first place she possessed a maternal antenna that was as delicate and as sensitive as a safecracker's fingertips. As if through some inborn radar system she could pick up the slightest change in the family atmosphere. In the second place there was her deep-seated passion to be a *behrya* (a competent housekeeper) which meant that she had the very special ability to keep things clean and to turn odds and ends into *meichulim* (tasty dishes). The Talmud makes it abundantly clear that "cleanliness is next to Godliness—carefulness leads to cleanliness, cleanliness to purity, purity to humility, humility to saintliness, saintliness to fear of sin, fear of sin to holiness and to immortality." And the Psalmist (51:10) added: "Create in me a clean heart, O God; and renew a steadfast spirit within me."

Preparing food was more difficult for her than for non-Jewish women because she had the added burden of worrying about the Mosaic dietary laws—about keeping the milk dishes separated from the meat dishes, for it is written in Leviticus (20:25, 26) "Ye shall therefore put difference between the clean beasts and the unclean beasts and between the unclean fowls and the clean: . . . And ye shall be holy to me, for I the Lord am Holy, and have separated you from other people, that ye should be mine." One must assume that the primary object of these laws was the promotion of health, although many will say that their purpose was basically to maintain an ideological superiority as a group distinction of the Jews. Actually the Torah nowhere declares these proscriptions to be hygienic in nature; nevertheless, all must agree that trichinosis is no respecter of time, place, or religious convictions. Be that as it may, the system of dietary laws is another example of those many specific ordinances which impose upon Jews responsibilities from which many other groups are free.

To the shtetl wife and mother these sociological arguments would mean nothing. All she knew was that the very food Jews ate set them apart as a people, made them different, superior, and sustained their character as the chosen of God; plus the fact that it protected her and her family from the diseases all around them and thus helped turn her home into a citadel in which she could perpetuate the Jewish faith.

If there was nothing else available she could always make chicken soup. She was convinced that chicken soup could solve any problem, not merely a problem of hunger but any problem. It would cure any disease, illness, or hurt, and would prove effective at weddings, as well as at funerals; but it was imperative at the Sabbath evening meal and at other holiday meals. If chickens had a history it would record strong distaste of the Jews and their philosophy of life, for they have been unwilling sacrifices for it for hundreds of years.

The shtetl homemaker had her own ideas regarding the treatment of illnesses. If chicken soup failed, she had other remedies and preventives which she had learned from her mother, who had learned them from her own mother before her. To be sure, some of them were based on sheer superstition, but sometimes they worked. Placing a goose quill filled with "quick silver" around the neck of a child would ward off most any "evil eye"; changing a sick child's name would fool the angel of death who might be hovering about;[7] pulling the left ear of a child when he sneezed would keep him from being stunted, and walking around a child rather than stepping over him would aid him in growing up tall and strong. Then there were al-

---

[7] The author recalls vividly the afternoon when his seven-year-old brother was critically ill, and he went searching for the *Treteur* whose job it was to change the individual's name so that God's timetable would be thrown off. The fee was thirty-five kopecs, in advance. However, either the practitioner's license had become invalid or the angel of death was not to be denied, because the handsome little boy died the same evening. It might be added, parenthetically, that even at nine years the writer had the feeling, albeit accompanied by some guilt, that this practice smelled just a little of hocus-pocus—but then one could not take a chance.

ways flaxseed and mustard poultices for chest pains, kerosene with sugar for colds, axle grease for bruises, and cobwebs for bleeding.

If all these failed and the *feltsher*, the semiskilled medical practitioner, could do no more, there was the inevitable and painful business of covering the mirrors in the house at the time of death.

In these times of sorrow the shtetl mother gathered strength from Job who himself knew the greatest of all sorrows (1:21). "The Lord gave, and the Lord hath taken away; blessed be the name of the Lord," he had said. She realized that at best "our days on the earth are as a shadow" (I Chron. 29:15) and she found solace in the sages who had written "whosoever labors in the Torah; as it is said 'From the gift of the law man attains to the heritage of God and by that heritage he reaches heaven.' " Indeed, her philosophy was simply that the dead must wait on the living and not the living upon the dead. When we are dead, only new life can hold on to what we hold dear. Love, courage, inspiration, a devotion to truth can be preserved only to a small degree in the written word, even in the Torah; they can best be preserved in the lives of the children who follow us. This was her doctrine of immortality, and she was not overly concerned with the metaphysical afterlife, for "thou will not abandon my soul to the nether world. Thou makest me to know the path of life." The path of life, that was the thing.

To the shtetl mother the path of life meant caring for her family, helping them achieve wholesome and well-adjusted personalities; it meant bringing to the family circle respect and confidence, mutuality and response, acceptance and expectations, support and stimulation, communication and simple personal friendship. The trouble was having enough time. She was always in need of more time, time to tell her children all the things they should know, more time to share with them the strength and hopes, more time to make them familiar with the blueprint of Jewish life, more time to impress upon them the nature of their destiny. Indeed, she needed more time to put together their hearts, minds, and souls.

Oftentimes when she looked upon her husband and children and saw their faces deeplined and haggard, her heart ached. Yet she also saw beneath those outward signs something subtle and fine and beautiful—a holy spirit shining through, binding her husband in emotion and dreams to God as did the leather straps of the phylacteries, guiding her son toward the way of the rabbi, and inspiring her daughter to be the wife of a scholar. Over and beyond the poverty she could feel the living spirit of love and righteousness reaching down into her family. Across the street, they called it the "Holy Ghost." Let them call it what they would—to her, it was God saying, "I am with thee."

If it took so much of her time, energy, and genius to care for her family, the shtetl wife needed more of these for another important duty—the business of hospitality in the home. In the shtetl there existed a unique type of hospitality—not merely the courtesy that is extended to another in a friendly home. This concept of hospitality was more a sort of spirit one showed to a stranger within his gates, be they the gates of his synagogue, his business, or particularly the gates of his home.[8]

This hospitality was a rare combination of courtesy, good will, affection, and charity, for God Himself judges the cause of the poor and needy. It is written "thou shalt love him [the stranger] as thyself; for ye were strangers in the land of Egypt: . . ." (Lev. 19:34). The Jews of the shtetl knew bitterly well what it meant to be strangers in a strange land; they knew what God meant when He admonished them: "For the land is mine; for ye are strangers and sojourners with me." (Lev. 25:23). Charity is one of the most highly developed concepts in Jewish life, and in the shtetl it was synonymous with justice, Tzedokah, and was actually considered a legal right. As a matter of fact, the ancient prophets had made it clear that as far as the Jews were concerned there is only one word for both charity and justice; thus charity to the poor is merely justice to the poor. The affliction of the poor is also Israel's affliction and God's concern. It

---

[8] Zborowski and Herzog, in their book *Life Is with People*, give a delightful and authoritative picture of charity in the shtetl. Philanthropy was continuously practiced by almost everybody as an everyday part of family, community, and religious life.

is written in Isaiah (41:17) "When the poor and needy seek water, and there is none, and their tongues faileth for thirst, I the Lord . . . of Israel, will not forsake them."

It was the conviction of the shtetl Jews that all who need must be cared for including "the Levite (because he hath no part nor inheritance with thee) and the stranger, and the fatherless, and the widow, who are within thy gates, shall come, and shall eat and be satisfied; that the Lord thy God may bless thee in all the work of thy hand which thou doest" (Deut. 14:29). Thus it was that the shtetl wife, in addition to aiding God in His handiwork through the medium of her family, made the meditations of her heart more acceptable in His sight by helping all those who came within the gates of her house and within the sanctity of her home.

Then the Lord God said: "It is not good that man should be alone, I will make him helper fit for him." The people of the shtetl took this piece of wisdom literally and the promise seriously, albeit they did not always trust God to find a "helper fit for him" so they created a *shadchun* whose purpose it was to help the Lord in the business of "making matches."[9] His has been a long a honorable profession. It began during the Crusades when much of Jewish community life in Western and Central Europe was uprooted or destroyed. There was great need to survive physically as well as spiritually and since endogamy was the law of Israel, it was imperative that the shadchun become an institution of a sort. It was an intriguing job but a delicate and difficult one. The business of going from one Jewish community to another in those days was, in itself, a precarious undertaking and the practice of acting as a "go-between" in the lives of young men and women whose hormones cared little for the laws of Moses or the sayings of the Fathers, called for artistry and discretion far beyond the ordinary. Indeed, it took a genius to

[9] Shadchun is a Yiddish term for marriage broker. The profession of matchmaking among Jews was already well established in the Middle Ages, at which time many rabbis and laymen made it a legitimate source of income and considered it a good and pious act.

bring together "a flea and an elephant," as the Yiddish expression has it.[10]

The shadchun worked hard for his fee, he was dedicated to his calling, and he contributed much to the family life of the shtetl. There marriage was carefully considered; for in a society conceived and organized around the family, the marriage contract was of supreme importance and the marriage ceremony of profound significance.[11]

In general, when a young man approached the age of marriage he found a set of clear-cut and religiously oriented ceremonies awaiting him. He made the acquaintance of available young women, with or without the aid of the shadchun, in a pleasant and inexpensive manner, but under the supervision of parents or other guardians of public morality. The young people were of the most possible homogeneous background. In the life of the shtetl there was little mobility, and most of the individuals who married were born and reared, literally, in homes next to each other.[12]

Parental control and little free choice were favored in respect to the courtship and marriage. The match was based, first of all, on the basis of the Jewish way of life rather than upon the caprice of personal love. This does not mean that the young people did not care for one another—it meant rather that they had been conditioned, since childhood, to look for the "right" person. Second, the match was based on social position and desire for security. Status was measured according to a dual standard: scholarship and economics, with scholarship, by far, outranking economic matters. No matter how poor a boy was, if he were learned in the Torah, pious, and upstanding according to the Jewish ideal, he would receive great recognition. As a matter of fact, if a man were wealthy and not learned he would

[10] Nathan Ausubel, *The Book of Jewish Knowledge* (New York: Crown Publishers, Inc., 1964), 398.

[11] Conrad Moehlman makes the interesting observation in his book *The Christian-Jewish Tragedy* that the early Christian fathers even went so far as to suggest that the marriage of Jacob constituted a symbol of the church. Lea, unattractive and weak, represents Judaism, while Rachel, the beautiful and the strong, represents the church.

[12] Willard Waller and Reuben Hill, *The Family* (New York: Dryden Press, 1956), 142.

gain special status by supporting the pursuit of scholarship. Oftentimes after the marriage arrangement was made the groom would obtain *kest* from his in-laws, that is, room and board, for a length of time in order that he may continue to study in peace. After marriage the couple might be supported by both sets of parents so that the son-in-law could continue his scholarly work.

Indeed, the couple in the shtetl attained a high degree of balance between romance and reality in the building of their marriage. Despite the fact that in the matter of the serious everyday events in their lives they could not afford the luxury of regarding marriage and family living through "romance"-colored glasses, they understood well the nature of the flesh and left to the flesh that which belonged to it. There simply could not be any halfhearted commitments regarding anything as vital as the family.

From a sociological point of view this attitude indicates a rare capacity of awareness regarding the purpose and goal of family living within a group whose *raison d'etre* was survival against great odds.[13] This awareness came to the surface every time a marriage was arranged. The marriage was a carefully discussed affair, in which the personal feelings of both partners were taken for granted, and the positive aspects of the contemplated relationship were carefully considered in consultation with all concerned. Albeit the prospective bride and groom both felt the pressure of the group, they were also aware that this process would result in a standard of behavior the ultimate purpose of which was to insure the survival of the group and thus the survival of their own family. Family tradition in the shtetl was rich and rewarding to a degree sufficient to stamp the individual with a family seal, yet not to hinder the development of his individual personality.

If the alliance was consummated it was customary that the bride's parents make every effort to give her *Nedunya* (a dowry), to which the wife had the title but of which the husband had the use.

---

[13] There is an old Jewish proverb which has it that "when a son marries he gives his wife a contract and his mother a divorce," a bit of very sound philosophy leading toward better marital relations then and now!

To be sure, every man must make an effort to marry the daughter of a man of character, for "as the tree is so is the fruit," also because "a good, a virtuous wife expands a man's character." And every woman must make an effort to marry a man of sound character, whose desire it is to respect and honor his wife, to care for his family, to study the Torah and to be a good Jew. And both had the dream that they would find mutuality as well as independence in their marriage.[14] But no matter who married whom, nor under what circumstances, the most important factor in the marriage was that young people marry in the faith. The shtetl people were never permitted to forget for one moment the Lord's commandment found in Numbers (36:6): "Let them be married to whom they think best; only to the family of the tribe of their father shall they be married."

To add emphasis to the business of marriage, it was traditional among the shtetl Jews that the rabbi be not only permitted to marry but practically impelled to do so. The rabbi was respected and loved, but no one removed hats for him, kissed his hands, or knelt in the streets for him. Because of his important position in the community and the degree to which he influenced the lives of his congregation his home became the center of Jewish culture and the model which other families must imitate.

Among most social groups the marriage ceremony takes on a special significance, and particularly was this the case among the shtetl Jews for whom the ritual carried with it particular meaning, value, and symbolism. Traditional Jewish marriage began with *Tenaim*, a binding agreement between the bride and the groom, comparable to becoming engaged.

On the day of the wedding, until after the marriage ceremony, both bride and groom were expected to fast to atone for their sins. The *Chathunah* (wedding ceremony) took place under a *chuppah* (canopy), often placed in the yard of the synagogue, and in the presence of two lawful witnesses, as well as friends and relatives. On the way to chuppah the couple was showered with raisins and almonds, or

[14] Actually, unsound marriages were discouraged by the rabbis; see Proverbs, 24:27.

with rice which signified the hope for happiness and productivity. The canopy is a reminder of the ancient tent-life of Israel. The person who solemnized the marriage (usually a rabbi, but not necessarily) recited the betrothal blessing in the traditional chant, whereupon the groom and bride sipped from a cup of wine after which they exchanged rings, reciting the formula which made them husband and wife: *"Harey at mekuddeshet li betabaat zo kedat mosheh ve-Yisroel"* ("Behold thou are consecrated unto me by this ring according to the Law of Moses and Israel)." The rings, incidentally, had to be smooth and round with no marks and no stones. The seven marriage benedictions—*sheva Berachoth*—were then said.

Throughout the entire ceremony appropriate music was played on the violin. The violin has for ages been claimed by Jews as their particular instrument. "This national affection for the violin," says Jerusalem critic-composer Yoharian Boehm, "stems from the days when the wandering Jews of Eastern Europe adapted the instrument from the gypsies." "The violin was inexpensive," says Boehm, "easy to carry and it could cry and sing like the human voice. So it best expressed the bittersweet emotions of the Jew in his homelessness."[15]

At the conclusion of this portion of the ceremony the groom and bride took a sip of wine again, from another cup. The ceremony was completed with the reading of the marriage contract—Ketubah—the bill of rights on which the marriage is based. After this the groom crushed a glass with his foot. This was symbolic of the sadness that always mingles with the happiness in life and reminded the couple as well as the guests of the tragedies in Jewish history and of the destruction of the Temple. After the wedding ceremony there was the usual banquet at which meal much stress was laid upon the twisted bread—*challah*—and upon chicken soup (to be sure).[16]

[15] "Music," *Time*, January 15, 1965, p. 49. Indeed the first rank of the world's best violinist is predominantly Jewish—David Oistrakh, Nathan Milstein, Leonard Kogan, Yehudi Menuhin, Jascha Heifetz, Isaac Stern. It is said that in Israel today, next to having a college professor in the family, the proudest parents are those who can boast about "my son the violin player."
[16] Abraham Z. Idelsohn, *The Ceremonies of Judaism* (Cincinnati: National Federation of Temple Brotherhoods, 1930), 127.

If the supreme tragedy occurred and a child married outside Judaism, the parents might regard the child as dead and engage in the ritual of mourning called "sitting shiva." This ritual of mourning included tearing their clothes and observing a ten-day mourning period of solemn prayer and seclusion from friends and even relatives. As primitive and as sad as the idea seems to be, it did have the tendency to keep individuals in the fold, to drive them back into the traditional family culture, or, in some cases, to drive them completely away from Judaism.

Despite the importance and sanctity assigned to marriage and family living, despite the deep and lasting symbolism involved in the union of two people in the Chathunah, despite the efforts made to hold the family together, and despite the fact that the Talmud says when a man divorces his wife not only the angels but the very stones weep, there were rare occasions when the marriage failed and the dreaded Get was inevitable. The word "Get" is Hebrew for "Writ of Divorce." Actually the Get is a document written in Aramaic, and the text is strictly prescribed by law.[17] Originally it was possible for a man to divorce his wife against her will; however, during the tenth century the divorce laws were changed with the stipulation that a wife may not be divorced without her consent. In the shtetl the rabbi had the authority to compel a man to give his wife a Get where such act was necessary and proper.

Some people have said that the shtetl mother "devoured" her children.[18] In a sense she did just that, just as God would devour His children, with the same fierceness and the same edelkeit (delicateness). The story of Job is an excellent example of this psychic process, and Job's excruciating confession of faith gives part of the answer to this paradox. "Though He slay me yet will I trust in Him."

[17] Even to this day the term "Get" carries with it a connotation for the writer which seems far more frightful than the term "divorce," although the end result is the same.

[18] The same thing is being said about the American Jewish mother as well. The Jewish best-seller, A Mother's Kisses, by Bruce Jay Friedman (New York: Simon and Schuster, 1964) is a good example. The mother in this novel is that stock figure, a "Yiddish mama" who devours her young.

Indeed, the shtetl mother overprotected and even overloved her child. She had reason to—it took her people thousands of years to make her child and to her he was that people. More than that, to her, in the last miserable Jewish child in the shtetl rested the future of all Judaism, yea, even the future of all mankind. Michelangelo, the great sculptor, never in all his glory of creating the immortal image of Moses out of marble was as inspired as the average Jewish mother of the shtetl was in her efforts to create the image of Moses in her son.[19]

The Jewish child in the shtetl was considered more than the mere result of the union of the parents, more than the sum of his ancestors; he contained another element, for he had been touched by the finger of God. It was believed, further, that he transmitted his Judaism generation after generation. Perhaps it was this belief that is responsible for the idea that Judaism is, somehow, a racial characteristic. By and large, in the shtetl the birthdays of children were not recorded; however in the case of a boy's birthday there was some effort to record it—by the family, so that it would know when he would be thirteen and thus be *Bar Mitzvah,* and by the government officials, so that they would know when he would be twenty-one and could be drafted into the army.[20]

To the people of the shtetl, the commandment "Be fruitful and multiply" meant far more than the simple affirmation of a command to produce children; to them it meant the release of the volcanic passions pent up in their hearts, minds, and souls; it meant the realization of their priceless opportunity to quicken forever the future course of Judaism in particular and of human progress in general. Those un-

[19] The well-known psychiatrist Harry Stock Sullivan observed that early family experiences are often quite subtle, and that almost from birth the mother, through empathy, communicates to the child such sentiments as love, hate, confidence, anxiety, and fear—all of which have a long run effect on personality. This process is termed "imprinting," by many psychologists. Harry Stock Sullivan, *Conception of Modern Psychiatry* (Washington: William A. White Foundation, 1947).

[20] The writer, for instance, was told by his mother that he was born *erev-pesach*—just before Passover. He arbitrarily chose May 10, when he came to America. It seemed like a pleasant day in the spring on which to be born.

sophisticated people believed that what they did with their children would influence what happened to all men, because they were convinced that every ideal which they cherished had sprung as though from some other person's heart and mind and it was their business to pass it on. Indeed, the shtetl parents were the rudder and the compass with which their children could go through life searching for further truth; for they had learned long before that unless truth is searched for, it does not come to light. There every child was welcome into the home despite the frightening counsel found in Genesis (3:16). "In sorrow thou shalt bring forth children." Indeed the shtetl parents preferred to go to Isaiah (60:22) for their counsel: "A little one shall become a thousand, and a small one a strong nation."

It is clear, then, that one of the most important goals Jews had in that particular community was to become parents and the most important job of every parent was to mold children into people—Jewish people—and these children became a heart-warming testimony to the strength of the unconquerable spirit found in the shtetl.

Every child, no matter where, is born into a world that already exists, but the shtetl child was born into a world that not only existed but was rigid in its norms and values, its discipline and purpose. There the child did not learn the ways of being a Jew through meeting the Jewish culture in the abstract; it was forced upon him, and fast, by his relatives, the people next door, and the neighbors across the street. It was they who knew and carried the patterns of Jewishness to him.

The ambition of all Jewish parents to see their sons grow up learned men and their daughters good homemakers and happily married is reflected even in the lullabies with which the shtetl mothers sang their children to sleep. None of that business of swinging a baby in the tree tops or filling its mind with fairy tales—here were songs visualizing the baby's future, his hopes and dreams, his joys and happiness. The following are examples of typical cradle songs for a boy and a girl:

Oh, hush thee, my darling, sleep soundly, my son,
Sleep soundly and sweetly till day has begun.
For under the bed of good children at night
There lies, till morning, a kid sunny white.
We'll send it to market to buy *sechora* (goods),
While my little lad goes to study the Torah.
Then you'll be a Rabbi when I have gone gray.
But I'll give you tomorrow ripe nuts and an toy.
If you'll sleep as I ask you, my own little boy.

Sleep, my birdie, close your eyes;
Sleep, oh sleep, my child, sleep with joy.
You know no sorrow, sleep with health, my child.
When, from your cradle, you will get up
There's plenty of work for you:
To embroider shoes, to read little books
But meanwhile sleep, my child.
When aside you will glance, young men will advance,
Handsome and of good address, their lives they will proffer.
And gifts will they offer;
But don't hasten to say "yes."
Your parents who love you, as a dowry will give you
Many thousands in cash.
Bride and groom, each then will kiss,
And we shall take part in your joy.
You will have a little one perfect and beautiful.
You will love it as I love you,
You'll kiss each little limb,
And you'll sing this song to him.
Sleep, oh sleep, my child.

Children who received such attention and affection all established early in life strong interpersonal ties with parents, siblings, relatives, and the community at large. By an infinitude of devices he was made to love his home and his religion. A good example of this is the fact that during many of the holiday rituals the child was the hero—particularly Passover, Chanukah, and the Bar Mitzvah services. This, perhaps, helps to explain the reason that although Jews in the shtetl were marginal people, treated as strangers and openly hated, few developed psychopathic personalities. A child in the shtetl could not be self-centered and his relation with others could not be self-centered or superficial. From the very beginning he was directed to internalize standards of right and wrong and be concerned with all those about him. He learned quickly that alone he was nothing—that only in relation to his family, his community, his group could he have meaning, value, and security.

Indeed, the expectations of the shtetl child were different from those of the non-Jewish child. No *mishmash* and no *pishpash*, he learned early in life that he was different, that he had a special purpose in life inherent in his being, that there would be times when hanging on would be the only dignity left to him, a condition which would cause him to be both hungry and ambitious, a predicament in which he strangely gloried despite the misery it brought. He learned, furthermore, that all men are sooner or later caught up in the net of good and evil—an idea which is both frightening and inspiring, and, finally he learned that it is better to follow even the shadow of the best rather than to remain content with the worst.

How did the shtetl child come to know and interpret this unique world of his? Simply by what he had been told and persuaded it was. His rigid and particular outlook on life and his simple humanity sustained his incredible hope in what appeared to be the dimmest of environments, and thus was his sight sharpened and his horizon extended.

To be sure, those people believed in miracles for, even as in biblical times, there were miracles in the shtetl the source of which was implied in the Shema and the manifestation of which was evident in the home. Thus was the strange alchemy of the shtetl home, a universe unto itself, and each child a microcosm reflecting the macrocosm which was that universe.

Outside the home there was the measureless sea, a world of rage and despair, of pain and trouble, of darkness and danger, but inside the home there was the pleasant and safe shore. Outside the house there was ever an atmosphere of something frightening and sad, a movement ever depressed and listless; inside there was a freshness and a peace. Even the outside of the average shtetl house was drab; time, sun, rain, and wind had covered those buildings with a grey color as though to reflect the grey soil under them and the pitiable structures seemed to make every effort to settle deeper into the grey Russian soil, crouching away from a world which kept them alien.

The material belongings of the shtetl Jews were few; most of them could not even own their homes. That was not new to them for nearly nineteen hundred years ago the Jewish historian Josephus observed: "Though we be deprived of our wealth, of our cities, of other advantages we have, our law, Torah, continues immortal." Even the poorest household had candlesticks for the Sabbath blessings; every male of age had his prayer shawl—the sacred *talis* which he received early in life and kept faithfully throughout his entire lifetime and in which he was eventually buried. Most families managed to obtain a samovar which was like a bottomless well serving up hot glasses of tea, morning, noon, and night. The most impoverished Jew found many occasions to say *lechayim* (your health) with wine or stronger beverages for "man is like a breath, his days are like a passing shadow." However, there must ever be sobriety among the shtetl Jews. They had to keep their wits about them, their judgment, their will power, their self-discipline. In fact, their early training helped to structure in their characters stable attitudes about drinking. If this were not enough, all they had to do was to look across the street and see what excess drinking can do to a people—indeed, there was ever that familiar and most uncomplimentary statement *"shekker ve a goy"* (drunk as a Gentile") to remind them. For the shtetl Jew, sobriety was a basic virtue—he, of all people, could ill afford to lose his self-control, his caution, his poise, and above all, his self-respect.[21]

To compensate for many shortcomings in that environment, there were ever the meichulim created in magic pots through some mys-

[21] Pittman and Snyder in discussing the drinking patterns of various groups, make this significant observation: "The drinking of alcoholic beverages is widespread among Jews and has been so since ancient times. In terms of percentages, there are probably more users of alcoholic beverage in the Jewish group than in any other major religio-ethnic group in America. Yet as has been shown repeatedly both in this country and abroad, rates of alcoholism and other drinking pathologies for Jews are very low." David J. Pittman and Charles R. Snyder (eds.), *Society, Culture, and Drinking Patterns* (New York: John Wiley and Sons, 1962), 188.

terious formula by the mother. The attention which the shtetl wife gave to cooking under all circumstances, sad or gay, was not purely hedonistic, rather it was somehow related to the idea of being civilized. And, if perchance, there were times when even the magic of pots created little the shtetl Jews used their vivid imaginations. While eating hard black bread and dried fish they bravely drew mental pictures of tables laden with challah, gefilte fish, chopped liver, wine, and, of course, chicken soup.

As a matter of fact, there have been some individuals who called the religion of the shtetl family a religion of pots and pans, referring to the emphasis placed on the ritual having to do with kosher and *traefe* (impure). The people of the shtetl would have answered this by saying that the whole business of *kashrus* (dietary laws) really has to do with self-discipline which, in turn, affects the entire character of the individual Jew as well as the group. There is still more to the kosher business. The shtetl Jews—short in stature, narrow chested, chronically undernourished, inbred, confined for centuries—were able to survive for psychological and sociological reasons, to be sure, but also because they followed closely the Mosaic code regarding matters of health in which food played a vitally important role.

There were always people visiting the shtetl home—relatives, friends, strangers, for Yose Ben Johanan, the sage of Jerusalem, had said: "Let thy house be opened wide and let the poor be members of thy household. . . ." There were always discussions, and every discussion sooner or later turned itself into a competitive examination covering the whole of the Torah. Intellectual discipline was a great virtue and was glorified by the family in the home as well as by the congregation in the shul. There is a delightful story told which may throw some light upon the nature of those discussions. Legend has it that Moses himself once came back to listen to a discussion of the Torah among a group of his followers who were visiting a Jewish home in the shtetl and did not recognize that it was his Torah they were discussing.

Thus it was that in the shtetl home Jews were prisoners—prisoners of God, prisoners of the Torah, prisoners of hope. They said their prayers in the morning and in the evening; they created meals as if by magic; they earned a living from the air; they considered their children treasures beyond measure; they continued on their pilgrimage through time and space with an unfaltering self-confidence, their lives permeated with the Messianic idea and with a passionate longing for the coming of the Messianic age, counting the days and years until a new star would come along which they could follow.

And suddenly a new star did come upon the horizon to the west, a star which reminded them of their vanished past and their hope of the future. It was the star which shone over America, the star which was reflected in the lamp held by the lady in the New York harbor.

So they packed their few belongings: their samovars, their candlesticks, their *talisim*, their prayerbooks, and they placed them in their wicker baskets. Their Hebraic inheritance they packed away in their hearts, minds, and spirits and they started again on their journey toward the everlasting hills, to that promised land where they might continue their unyielding effort of immortality which to them meant that stability, that permanence, that unique quality of the soul which, if lost, left nothing worthwhile preserving in this world.

They came by the thousands—the young and the old, the strong and the weak, the brave and the frightened—their thoughts so interwoven into their dreams that they did not know where one ended and the other began, *la kiddush hashem*—for the sanctification of God's name.

VII

How the Mighty Have Fallen

So they came through this golden door by the tens of thousands, these *challuzim*—pioneers of the spirit—to seek a new frontier; in some ways alike, in some ways strangers, but their destination was ever the same. Between 1880 and 1914 about two million Jews came from Eastern Europe to America. They came searching for those everlasting hills, looking far back and looking far ahead, filled with reverence and faith for the star that was shining in the cool sky of the west. They saw the shore only dimly, and they imagined it to be beautiful as well as sound, and a feeling of mystery and joy touched their hearts, agonizing in its intensity. In the breaking dawn of their arrival the new land appeared tender and loving; everywhere there was light and kindness, excitement and happiness. Here was a new world waiting for them—a world of fascinating adventure and endless promise. Here were hopes as yet unborn and here were pains as yet unknown. How enchanting America looked to those shtetl Jews, how fragrant was the springtime of their coming, how incredible the distant roar of the cities, and how unbelievable the strange colors of the prairies, how remote the sights and sounds of the desert, and how frightful the shadows and odors of the swamps. One must not take this attitude lightly. It was the beautiful hour before their world would grow old and shadowy around them. It was a day without doubt and fear, a time full of wonder and anticipation.

They went beyond the cities and the prairies, beyond the deserts and swamps. All the way from Boston to San Francisco, from Lafayette, Louisiana, to Walla Walla, Washington, one can trace Jewish footsteps. And everywhere they went they left monuments eloquently testifying to their hard work, their devotion to justice, their passion for freedom, their belief in America, and their love for God. This is not to imply that Jews have been only on the giving end of the relationship with America. They have received as much or more than they gave. The reciprocal influence in this case makes a dramatic tale in itself.

By this qualitative leap these prodigious wayfarers of the world came into a new land, and it seemed as though fate had at last caught up with them and had once again answered the plea of Moses: "Let my people go."

Surely one of the most magnificent moments in the life of this writer was the one when he first saw the Statue of Liberty. He can still recall the scene vividly and with an all but overpowering tenderness and excitement. He was standing on the deck of the ship in the very early morning looking toward the New York Harbor, straining to see into the apocalyptic day for which he had been waiting so long. Suddenly the fog was lifted as if by some magic hand, and the clouds fell apart as the wind pushed them this way and that way, and the sun came streaming across the bay. There was first the water below, like liquid amethyst changing and glancing with the dazzling rays, and as his eyes slowly moved up, a curious sense of quiet suddenly fell over his personal world—a quiet which is difficult to explain, for there he saw the "Lady with the Lamp" standing at the golden door. The wonderful Lady and the strange little boy talked to each other, not just across the bay, not just across the harbor, but across the stream of time. On that bright morning he could see forever.

It is a painful reality and an inescapable fact that when a person or a people move on they leave things behind them. What did the shtetl Jews leave behind them? Did they leave something of themselves, perhaps, something of their hearts, minds, and spirits as Jews have always left behind them in their wanderings? Only history will disclose what they left and to what degree this abandonment will influence their destiny.[1] But no matter what was left behind or what was brought along, transplanted to American soil those vigorous seedlings from the shtetl took root and flourished.[2]

For several generations these refugees used the creative source of their philosophy and love of God, their drive for freedom, and justice, and their recognition of social equality, and the deep sense of humility of their prophets to make Judaism and everyday living coextensive. During these years there were burning problems. There were slums and there was child labor; there were self-imposed ghettoes like the East Side in New York and the West Side in Denver; there was the painful business of climbing up the social and economic ladder, and of shedding many of the old garments, physical, economic, and psychical. Nevertheless, these people were convinced that they were about to fulfill the age-old promise of freedom and peace and enter again into the spirit of the traditions and idealisms of ancient Judaism.

Most Jews in America believed sincerely that they could build an ideal Jewish community in the new land which would, at least, resemble the community once portrayed by Professor Israel Friedlaender. He perceives "a community great in number, mighty in power, enjoying life, liberty, and the pursuit of happiness: true life,

---

[1] There is a Jewish legend which has it that all fragments left behind during the Jewish wandering over the earth, God Himself secretly gathers up in one bundle and takes to the land of Israel where He saves them until the end of time. It may well be that in America God will finally pick up the last fragments of Judaism.

[2] There has been much written on the topic of Jewish life in America at the turn of the century. However, from this writer's point of view there are two works of particular value, one a historical analysis and the other fictional. Both take a voyage through time and space to an atmosphere once well known but now only dimly remembered. The first is *The Promised City*, by Moses Rischin (New York: Corinth Books, 1964), a turbulent story of Jewish life in New York between 1870 and 1914, honestly seen and ably written. The second is *Call It Sleep*, by Henry Roth (New York: Avon Books, 1964) a truly American classic portraying the struggle of a sensitive Jewish child growing up on the East Side.

not mere breathing space; full liberty, not mere elbow room; real happiness, not that of pasture beasts; actively participating in the civic, social, and economic progress of the country, freely sharing and increasing its spiritual possessions and acquisitions, doubling its joys, halving its sorrows; yet deeply rooted in the soil of Judaism, clinging to its past, working for its future, true to its traditions, faithful to its aspirations, one in sentiment with their brethren wherever they are, attached to the land of their fathers as the cradle and resting place of the Jewish spirit; men with straight backs and raised heads, with big hearts and strong minds, with no conviction crippled, with no emotion stifled, with souls harmoniously developed, self-centered and self-reliant; . . . a community such as the Prophet of the Exile saw in his vision: 'And marked will be their seed among the nations, and their offspring among the people. Everyone that will see them will point to them as a community blessed by the lord.' "[3]

For a time the American Jews believed they were on the way of establishing a rather good example of the Utopia painted by Professor Friedlander. They achieved remarkable success in many areas of life. Given the great opportunities found in America, they used their intellect, courage, motivation and chutzpeh (gall) to forge far ahead of most other immigrant groups. They became leaders in the labor movement (but not in the mining industry), in the field of medicine (but not in banking), in law (but not in public utilities), in social work (but not in insurance), in entertainment (but not in transportation). They even moved away from New York's East Houston Street and Denver's West Colfax Avenue. They built beautiful temples and social centers and trained a new type of rabbi. They became members of clubs rather than lodges, and they played golf whereas their fathers played cards. As a matter of fact, they are really no longer marginal people, politically or economically, and are now rather well accepted by their Christian counterparts, the middle-class Protestants, who think they are a pretty good lot. (They ought to, for Jews have spent millions of dollars and used millions of words in

[3] Isaac B. Berkson, *Theories of Americanization* (New York: Teachers' College, Columbia University, 1920), 96.

their effort to educate Christians so that Christians will think better of them.) And finally they have reached a special height in status, for today when the American Jew is buried he is immortalized for his material success, whereas his grandfather was merely immortalized for his spiritual success.

However, along the way they picked up new fragments, perhaps to replace those they left behind. They found other gods, they heard new voices, they exchanged the old prophets for new ones, they began to generate new creeds and to follow untried doctrines. In short, in their eagerness to conform, to be more American than everybody else, to become emancipated, to shed every vestige of the shtetl, they "threw out the baby with the bath water." Thus it was they woke up one morning to find that the Jewish scene in America had changed with a vengeance. It must be made clear at this point that the writer is not *schrien gewald*—"yelling help! help!"—that he is not a prophet of doom on the one hand nor a Pollyanna on the other. It is this writer's purpose here not to recite all the worst things in the American Jewish scene, nor to refute them. Neither does he wish to minimize the shortcomings in Jewish life today which must be obvious to any thinking Jew. It is his business to try to state things as they are and not as they should be, without any antagonism or blissful serenity, not too loudly but more in a whisper, coupling disciplined intelligence with an active imagination and a deep optimism with a personal knowledge of some shadowy places in the American Jewish soul. In short, the writer hopes he is making a bold, hardheaded analysis of the Jewish situation in America, admitting quite frankly that he has a passionate concern over Judaism and its future and that he wishes to be an intimate part of it today and hopes that his daughter and her family will be a part of it in years to come. He may not be very elegant in his portrayal of the situation, but he believes with Albert Einstein: "If you are out to describe the truth, leave elegance to the tailor."

The ambiguities of life among the American Jews today echo the opening lines of *A Tale of Two Cities*: "It was the best of times, it was the worst of times." It is the best of times because it is marked by personal freedom, a high standard of living, opportunities beyond their forefathers' wildest dreams; it is the worst of times because it is also a time when the threat of disintegration, extinction, and, most important, psychic emptiness hangs heavily over the heads of the American Jewish people.

There is a painful bit of irony involved in the American Jewish scene. Sinai, the fountainhead of a great faith, once rose from the desert wilderness to look down upon a host of ignorant, homeless slaves and show them the road away from physical slavery and toward spiritual freedom. Today Sinai, the symbol, still looks down upon a horde of people, not homeless and not slaves, but quite civilized, refined, educated, free—yet equally lost in the maze of a modern desert wilderness.

This wilderness is not geographic in nature but spiritual. It seems to be spreading over the land in ever widening circles, engulfing most people in America; the most tragic thing about it is that it contains indefinable and intangible dangers. In an effort to escape this spectre, individuals bury themselves deeper in material comfort and mental complacency. The weariness of such a life, the hollowness of its mechanical joys, the burdens of its worldly cares and fears, the guilts and insecurities, the stresses and strains which accompany them, are narrowing our reality of life to whatever can be measured, calculated, constructed, and touched. Many children today are confused for they no longer know what to believe; around them there is too little ethical insight, too little genuine generosity, too little love, care, spiritual strength, and sound direction. It seems hardly possible that such conditions as these can continue without bringing some kind of tremendous upheaval, some kind of maddened behavior, some kind of fear from which the spirit, mind, and heart of man can escape without hitherto unknown results. It goes without saying that neither as individuals, as religious groups, nor as a nation can we long survive these conditions.[4]

---

[4] Despite this somber view, the writer has a love for America that is wordless, simple, and deep. He sees America as a very special place in the world of nations and as a very noble idea among the philosophies of men.

Oddly enough, the source of this social malady is not as yet generally understood, but it manifests itself in a widespread mood of anxiety and deep disquietude of the spirit which is sensed oftentimes rather than expressed.

Where do the American Jews find themselves standing in the miasma of discontent which has spread over the land? The answer is as unpleasant as it is complicated, for since American Jews have lost the simple traditional patterns of life and have become an intimate part of the inordinate complexity of the artificial and sensate civilization around them, the universe of their grandfathers has shrunk to a petty space not much larger than their smug communities, egocentric, materialistic, and nervous.

The life pattern of American Jews in recent years has largely fostered the "success pattern," with its emphasis upon tangible achievements: income, the right profession, the proper address, the prestige club, compromise—in short, an intense effort to outdo their counterparts in the American middle class. As a matter of fact, Jews are in the middle class of the middle class in the American social structure.[5] In a sense this is understandable since the middle class is the safest place to be, economically, politically, and socially. However, the psychic implications of this condition are enormous. Once Jews reigned as lords and masters of their own creation; now this is no longer true. In a world which they have created and made to operate on other men's terms, to what and to whom can they turn for strength and guidance, for inspiration, and for hope? There is a terrible price to pay for such transfer of allegiance. Here, then, is a strange twist of fate. Whereas the Jews of the shtetl were slaves to the past, to superstition, to rigid rules and patterns, the modern sophisticated Jews in America are also, in a sense, slaves to conformity, to gadgetry, to the compulsion to be like everyone else. Jews in America learn history well but not the lesson of history. They have forgotten that one of the basic reasons for their survival has been that they "think otherwise, and remain otherwise." Jews are different, say what you will,

[5] George E. Simpson and J. Milton Yinger, *Racial and Cultural Minorities* (New York: Harper and Brothers, 1953), 348.

believe what you will. This is not necessarily a mere chauvinistic slogan—being different does not necessarily imply being better or being worse—it simply means being unlike other people. Of course, Jews are different and in this simple assertion may be found the riddle of the Jews.

Here is a strange paradox. In order to remain Jewish one must be different, but as long as one is different he will stand apart. This contradictory reality may be in some way related to the Judaic concept of truth. The absolute truth represented by the Divine Law is inaccessible in full even to the most powerful human intellect. Each word in the Torah has, according to ancient tradition, four kinds of meaning: the direct, the interpreted, the allusive, and the secret. It may be that in the light of this approach to the truth there will never be a final answer to the Jewish dilemma.

It is the same old story all over again, Jews simply must have a "something more" if they are to survive, and that "something more" cannot be measured in terms of wealth, position, or gadgets. It rests in the measure of men, women, and children.

This sociopsychological fact may be unpleasant and undesirable, even tragic, but Jews can no more escape from it than they can escape from their shadows and remain in the light of day. This is their fate, and they cannot abstract themselves from it merely by wearing dark glasses. The sooner this special characteristic of Jewish life is recognized, the sooner Jews will be able to adjust to this condition.

Sometimes one gets the impression that Jews in America are mere patrons of their own old traditions, their special religious convictions, their unique goals in life, and their past dedications, like spectators at a baseball game who watch the action out in right field. Obviously such grotesqueries cannot be endured very long in a world of tumultuous confusion such as we live in today without some serious decadence invading the heart, mind, and soul of the individual. Indeed, Judaism is still a living faith; it is still deeply entrenched in the culture of most of western society. But there are signs that it is slowly disintegrating from the dry rot with which its theology, rabbis, and congregations have been stricken. The burning idealism, the passionate and uncompromising fight for righteousness and human dignity, the vehement determination to make Judaism and everyday living coextensive seem to have been dissipated in the struggle for conformity and for technological progress. This effort seems to have left many Jews spiritually and psychically exhausted and has resulted in an apparent impotence of the Judaic *neshoma* (soul). And the result? An enormous vacuum at the center of Jewish life. If this trend continues, the end is inevitable: it will be "ethno-suicide."

Indeed, what will be the "end"? Paul Kresh, editor of *American Judaism*, paints a dramatic, thought-provoking, and painful picture of that "end" with a skill that is rare, a courage to be envied, and an insight that is unique. Here follows a précis of his editorial:

When they decided to open the Museum of Living Judaism to the public on Saturdays and put me on exhibit I was a little embarrassed at first but after I got the hang of it I didn't mind so much. . . . It is a lonely life and I do not understand what I did to deserve it. Wasn't I always a good Jew? Was it my fault if my children deserted the reservation and married outside the faith? . . . I don't understand what went wrong. When I was a boy, there were five Jewish families in America and people treated us with kindness and respect. They said we had given the Bible and a code of morality to the world, and that was a good thing. My parents told us our religion was 'living Judaism,' but if it was so alive it is so strange that so few practiced it. Once nearly three percent of the country's population was Jewish. By the year 2000 it was down to 1.6 percent, although there were still five and a half million Jews. But the number went down. . . . A thoughtful government placed us on reservations to protect us, like the buffalo. When only I remained they put me on display in the museum. Now I am invisible, inaudible. The vanishing Jew has vanished. . . . What did it? Birth control? Intermarriage? Loss of identity? Lack of commitment? Rejection of the concept of peoplehood? Assimilation? Inability of the synagogue and its institutions to make Judaism truly *Live*? Disunity? Failure of leadership, of Jewish education, or worship forms, of sense of history, of transmission of values of an age-old heritage? Why did 'love' succeed where 'hatred' failed? Why didn't we enjoy our Judaism when we were free to observe its precepts, to practice it, to live it? Why didn't we cherish the poetry, the beauty, the drama, the balance, the meaning and direction it offered our lives? . . . How shall I carry out my mission to be 'a light unto the nations,' alone like this—unseen, unheard? . . . My God, my God, why have we forsaken you?[6]

This is indeed a grim and tragic picture and a most ignoble ending to the drama which is the story of Judaism. Could it happen? Indeed it could, but it does not have to happen, says Rabbi Maurice N. Eisendrath in his timely book on Jewish survival.[7]

The author believes that the answer is so simple that most Jews cannot grasp its meaning or its implications. The answer is a return to "Jewishness." Here is the crowning irony of the Jewish situation in America: Jewishness is disappearing from the lives of Jews. Once Jewishness produced Jews. Today it is the other way around—Jews produce such Jewishness as they possess and it is quite artificial. This paradox is one of the outstanding qualities in the life of American Jewry. They want desperately to remain Jews, yet they want equally to be just like their neighbors. Despite the fact that many of them have achieved these ends, deep down they nevertheless feel incredibly remote. It has become clear to most thinking Jews that from now on a mere decorative Judaism is not enough, even for one's personal existence in this world. The faith must be an actual faith, meaningful, practical, and living. To believe in God and in Judaism must mean to live in such a manner that life could not possibly be lived if God and Judaism did not exist. Then only can the earthly hope of Jews become a real force in their own lives and in the lives of other men. They feel this but somehow they do not possess the strength, courage, motivation to do something about it.

They know in their souls, for example, that they should be proud of their rabbis who have the courage to go to St. Augustine, Florida, but they are ashamed of them; they know in their bones that they should respect their co-religionists who stand up against the demagogues in Mississippi, but they are embarrassed by them; they "know in their hearts" that what went on in a cow palace in the summer of

[6] Paul Kresh, editorial, *American Judaism*, XIII (Summer, 1964), 5. Reprinted here with the kind permission of Mr. Kresh.

[7] Maurice N. Eisendrath, *Can Faith Survive?* (New York: McGraw-Hill Book Co., 1964).

1964 was not too far removed from what went on in a beer hall in 1932, yet they approved of it. The result of all this inner conflict is a keen frustration and an incomplete acceptance of life, a combination of resentment and resignation. Indeed, many modern sophisticated and completely emancipated Jews find that their tall shadows fall across their sleep and bring them nightmares. It is a painful observation to make, but it could be that throughout America today the hands of Esau are more in evidence than the voice of Jacob.

In the final analysis Jews in America face the same old story over again—a story made new. It is again a matter of "en berayrah" for Jews, be they Americans, Russians, Germans, or Israeli, be they New Yorkers, Texans, Alabamans or "Cajuns" from Louisiana. To be sure, there is a very slight choice—the choice between the security which blinds one and the responsibilities which awaken one.

An awakening is the key—an awakening to the Hebraic foundations which are so basic in Jewish life because of the extraordinary reality of the Jewish character. Will it always have to be true that only when some tyrant spreads darkness over the earth the strength of Judaism increases?

Jews in America no longer recognize themselves. "The questions 'Who am I?' and 'What am I?' are rendered almost unbearable for the contemporary American Jew."[8] Most American Jews feel a sort of claustrophobia about their religion; it presses down on them from all directions, and so they want to escape from it. They see it simultaneously as a priceless heritage and as a dead albatross around their necks. Theirs is a poignant tale of a people groping for a faith, trying to make rhyme and reason out of being Jewish. American Jews are discovering that they, of all people, cannot live according to a philosophy of "as if"[9] without getting involved in a hodgepodge of

[8] Bernard Rosenberg and Gilbert Shapiro, "Marginality and Jewish Humor," *Midstream*, IV (Spring, 1958), 80.

[9] H. Vaihinger, *The Philosophy of 'As if'* (New York: Harcourt, Brace and Co., 1925), viii. Vaihinger describes this principle: "An idea whose theoretical untruth or incorrectness, and therefore its falsity, is admitted, is not for that reason practically valueless and useless: for such an idea, in spite of its theoretical nullity may have great practical importance."

intellectual and emotional inconsistencies which for them can only end in psychic disaster, for it would mean they would not only lose sight of the destiny of things but of the origin of things as well. Jews cannot live as if they have no history, no faith, and no body of convictions. Perhaps it would be better if they had no history, for it has been wisely said that a people who have no history are a happy people. As far as Jews are concerned this is nonsense, for they do have a history and a long one.

Stored up in their group life is ever the hint of memory covering an area as far as the horizons can reach, beyond the desert, beyond the hills, beyond the mountains, emanating from all those anonymous spirits who lie buried along the way from Ur to Canaan and Egypt to Palestine, to Greece, to Rome, to Spain, to Poland and to Russia. It has been this power that spurred them on during the ages. "Is there such a thing as an ancestral memory?" is an intriguing question. Many Jews in America and the world over believe that there must be, else how do they get that "feeling" albeit they know next to nothing about Judaism. There is no real mystery here, there are no inexplicable miracles. It is just that Jews, no matter where they go, can see all around them contents of their unique treasure chest. Small wonder the memory is kept alive, no matter what!

Theirs is a memory spun of a thousand strands of ideas and dreams, tragedies and glories, sunshine and darkness. It has been this group memory which was really responsible for the miracle of the Jews throughout history. The American Jews do not stop to reason that if their forefathers had actually practiced a philosophy of life like that which flourishes in their midst today, they themselves would never have arrived at this point in history.

"Will the Jews continue to exist in America? Any estimate of the situation based on an unillusioned look at the American Jewish past and at the contemporary sociological evidence must answer flatly— no," says the well-known Rabbi Arthur Hertzberg, historian, sociologist, and writer on Jewish topics.[10] It is impossible to ignore such a

[10] Arthur Hertzberg, "The Present Casts a Dark Shadow," *Jewish Heritage* (Winter, 1963–64), 12.

bold statement on the part of even one rabbi, and many of his colleagues agree with him. The reason why this may be so may be
found in the drift of circumstances surrounding Jewish life today. At
this point in American Jewish history Jews find themselves at a sort
of crossroads. The flow of ancient Hebraic tradition and the modern
American way of life seemed to mingle their waters smoothly and
successfully for a time, but sooner or later one channel will have to
be established through which the dominant life stream will run. Jews
cannot fervently embrace the host culture which, without question,
offers them an abundance of material success, safe anonymity, middle-
class security, quiet tranquilization, and spiritual euthanasia while at
the same time holding on to those bedrock presuppositions which
through four thousand years of history have made Judaism a going
concern and helped its people survive against unbelievable odds.
Furthermore, these presuppositions fermented the ideas which evolved
the principles stressed in the Ten Commandments and subsequently
in Christianity, the Declaration of Independence, the ideals of equality and brotherhood. To remain in this precarious position will, sooner or later, leave Jews spiritually and psychically exhausted, and they
will not only lose faith in their own Messiah but in the American
"Messiah"—Progress—as well. At that time New York City will
have that new archeological museum open to the public on Saturdays, "The House of Living Judaism," administered by a group of
curious people then referred to, oddly enough, as the "Wandering
Christians." It is indeed ironical that there is a point in the existence
of an individual, a religious group, or even an entire nation when life,
having showered us with genuine pearls as gifts, begins to exact our
life's blood for paste.

Jews began struggling with God a long time ago, when Jacob first
wrestled with the angel and said to him: "I will not let thee go except
thou bless me." As long as they struggled with Him, argued with
Him, disagreed with Him, they knew Him. During the ages God's
words came to the Jews now with compassion, now with bitterness,
now with terror and now with joy, now with accusation and now with
assertion, but they came. Today in America the Jews no longer strug-

gle with Him, nor argue, nor even disagree with Him, and so His
voice is all but silent. It is not really that the modern American Jew
is less pious than his grandfather; it is, rather, that piety has changed
directions—it has changed from a dimension of depth to a horizontal
dimension. Many American Jews quite frankly question whether the
God of their fathers has anything really to say to the modern American scene. They wonder if there is anything in biblical and rabbini-
cal tradition which is applicable in these days when there are available so many panaceas for man's troubles on television and radio,
in newspapers and magazines, at store counters. Then, too, there is the
problem of hearing God's voice amidst the noise of our fastmoving,
bloated culture, filled with the deafening sounds of superhighways,
space ships, and the daily rise and fall of the stock market.

Religion has become a faraway, faint echo in the hearts of many
Jews today as compared to what it once was. They no longer feel the
urgency of religion as did the Jews of the shtetl; what was once a
passion has now become a convention. Far too many Jews have no
practice of religion and have only the vaguest idea of what is meant
by God or by living according to the ideals of Judaism. When they
need strength and inspiration for the living of this day they find
nothing to turn to. They experience the sensation felt by the Russian cosmonaut who, while circling in the heavens, looked out to see
God and saw nothing at all. This is quite understandable and an old,
old story, for when man trusts nothing but his own powers and resources he soon becomes hopelessly lost in the infinite void of a silent and faceless world. This becomes a most vicious cycle for the
more he loses spiritual security the more he rushes to the only thing
he still has left—the apparent security which can be created at will
and purchased over the counter.

Moses must have been an astute psychologist for in his farewell
address he reminded the wandering Jews of another age that "man
does not live by bread alone," and he might have added, nor by
"mink" alone. "And he humbled thee, and suffered thee to hunger,
and fed thee with manna, which thou knewest not, neither did thy
fathers know; that He might make thee know that man doth not live

by bread only, but by every word that proceedeth out of the mouth of the Lord doth man live" (Deut. 8:3).[11]

The most significant feature of the problem facing American Jews is essentially one of the spirit. American Jews of today, with their practical-mindedness on the one hand and their recent intellectual ascendance on the other, shy away from the perplexity of the spiritual. They cannot get their hands on it. It is not something to be added in an accounting book, or measured by a yardstick, or timed by a clock. In consequence they avoid and evade it. One example of this strange ambivalence regarding Judaism is expressed in the following statement made by a colleague of the writer at his university, a young and most competent student of political science who married a lovely young woman of his faith in a synagogue only a short time ago and who is now searching for truth among the Quakers.

Having had a rather thorough education and participation in Judaism, I feel somewhat qualified to comment on my personal relationship with Judaism and its shortcomings in meeting my own spiritual needs (and possibly, the needs of others).

To consider Judaism's failings without involving the other major religious faiths in the United States is, I feel, doing an injustice to Judaism. For Judaism as practiced in America, although it may possess singular assets and liabilities of its own creation, can be easily compared to Roman Catholicism and the majority of Protestant sects. It is important to point out that I am speaking partly of theological doctrines, but mostly of the practices of the three major religious faiths.

It seems to me that these religious bodies fail to provide for the individual needs and creativity of their members. Much of this problem lies in the maintenance and glorification of ritual. While providing a dramatic effect and satisfying the individual's need for the security to be found in repetition, the use of ritual and the dogmatic insistence upon form severely limits the ability of the worshipper to communicate and find his connection with God. Prayers, poems, and liturgy—which once may have carried and embodied the utmost meaning to their individual authors and composers—are reduced to meaningless words in a mechan-

---

[11] Obviously manna here meant more than physical bread, rather a heavenly bread for which man longs because it feeds his spirit.

ical recitation. The situation becomes even more distressing in a Jewish service when congregants, many of whom haven't the slightest understanding or notion of what they're saying, mumble Hebrew prayers.

Most organized religions provide for the necessary collective, group participation, but neglect the need for individual prayer and meditation. The paternal function of religion, which in itself is positive, should create an atmosphere in which people can move in their own directions within the larger, collective framework rather than being led like cattle, *en masse*. In the present situation, creative and unique attempts to communicate with God and one's self are not only discouraged but also stifled by this structural rigidity.

Another aspect of the problem facing religion in America today is its failure to bring spiritual values into the secular world. Most organized religions focus their attention on the Sabbath, and while worshippers pay lip service, in many cases, to the theological principles on Friday night or Sunday morning, they most often neglect them on the other days of the week. Attending a religious service and belonging to a religious congregation, regardless of the denomination, have come to be social necessities in the 1960's, an act required by etiquette and social mores, thereby turning the spiritual center into a fashion-conscious, conversation-oriented community center. Correspondingly, the clergyman's role has shifted from that of spiritual leader to that of friend, counselor, administrator, public relations man, and so forth.

Finally, one must regrettably take notice of the participation by most American religious groups in the race for material rather than spiritual gains. In trying to keep up with the goals of their members, (e.g., "keeping up with the Joneses") churches and synagogues have found themselves involved in a contest for status and prestige within the community. One form of this concern has been labeled the "edifice complex," wherein a congregation's preoccupation with appearance and the opinion of others leads it to spend vast sums of time and money on its "exterior." Therefore, the inner, spiritual concerns of the congregation are neglected in deference to the more outward, secular concerns.

I realize that it's impossible to make valid generalizations about every congregation or every religious person, but these characteristics seem to be widespread in religious congregations throughout the nation. Thus, they present a problem (at least, in my own view) of the utmost gravity and a situation which has neither met nor fulfilled my personal needs.

Many angry young men like him are becoming frightened because they are discovering to their dismay that in their eagerness to become like everyone around them they have gone to perilous extremes to eliminate these religious characteristics which brought them to where they are today—in short, they are finding that Judaism is becoming a religion of "normality." Many of them realize that the modern space age has taken away some of the confidence they used to have when they spoke about the unshakability of the eternal hills. But as far as the earth itself is concerned, hills are still about as permanent as any aspect of the landscape and, symbolically, they still stand for something certain. These hills can still say to mankind in the words of George Santayana: "Blow what winds would. The ancient truth was mine."

Contemporary confusion in American Judaism has increased to the point of bedlam over the matter of certainty. There seems to be a blur in the Jews' vision regarding their religious philosophy. Two facts account for this upheaval. The first is that Judaism has been organized for thousands of years around some great assurances and some basic certainties which brought unity, direction, and integrity to life. Though the rest of the world should slip into a sea of darkness, these truths were regarded as absolute and immutable. The second fact is that many American Jews seem to be losing these assurances and certainties and are suffering from "anomie"—loss of orientation. When the average Jew today faces a crisis, he cannot say with the depth of feeling and sincerity what his grandfather could: "This I know for sure!" What do American Jews know, religiously speaking? At best their religion has become a fragmentation of interests. The result is that they become all locked up on the inside; they feel that spiritually they have been robbed, robbed of the meaning of life and the reason for living; they continue to equivocate about their Judaic values and to be afraid, even to show any concern over what might happen to their grandchildren.

Dr. Stuart Rosenberg relates a popular folktale of the Old World Jew which describes poignantly the condition of so many American Jews.[12] A young Jew from the shtetl could no longer tolerate the

[12] Stuart E. Rosenberg, *America Is Different* (New York: Thomas Nelson and Sons, 1964), 247.

persecution around him so he fled to Germany, changed his name and religion, went to the university and became a very "successful" citizen. Years later his old father searched him out. After listening to his son's glowing account of his success, prestige, *and wealth*, the old man asked one question: "You have all these wonderful things, and that is good, but tell me, throughout all this is there anything left to remind you that you are a Jew?"

"Oh, nothing," answered the son, "but wait, there is one thing I still remember."

"And what is that?" the father wanted to know.

"Remember, father," he replied, "how night after night when I would run home from cheder in our shtetl, I had to pass the house of many Christians and every night as I passed, their dogs would bark? Remember, father, how afraid I was of those barking dogs? Well, father, even now whenever dogs bark I am afraid."

American Jews still hear dogs barking and they still fear them. This writer still has a painful feeling in the pit of his stomach when he hears dogs barking in the dark, for it reminds him of the barking he heard when he ran home from the cheder. To be sure, the writer is now safe, he can lock his doors, he knows the chief of police personally, the mayor's wife is a former student of his, he and the sheriff are on very friendly terms, but deep down he is never quite certain that some night a cross will not be burned on his front lawn. Imagine, a cross burning on a Jewish lawn. Indeed, "how odd that God would choose the Jews!"

Dr. Rosenberg sums up this dramatic situation most ably when he says: "For Jews, America is different. . . . And yet certain fundamental vestiges remain embedded in the depths of the Jewish psyche. In America, as elsewhere in the long history of their Diaspora, psychologically, Jews are still in exile." Then he offers the pathetic clincher to the whole business by quoting from Irving Howe: "He, (the American Jew) has inherited the agony of his people; its joys he knows only second hand."[13]

[13] *Ibid.*, 247.

This is understandable, for the grandparents in the shtetl had certainties which often seem no longer valid in this day: that the past deserved their respect, the present, their devotion, and the future, their hope. To their grandparents life was meaningful and worth struggling for; religious affiliation was more than a matter of personal preference. As the American Jew looks about him, evaluates his ideals and purposes, weighs his goals in life, he has the suspicion that along the way someone has stolen his birthright. It may well be said that American Jews are excellent examples of man in his loneliness searching for something amid the confusion of his world.

One must not assume that it will be easy to arrest this flight from religion in general and from Judaism in particular. Distortions, illusions, and rationalizations can be very precious and comforting to many Jews. The trouble with this sort of outlook is that if one leans long enough on these elements they may be all one has left. Many modern American Jews have simply lost their God and the safety with Him. There is an inescapable fact about fallen gods—they do not fall a little; they crash and shatter, and the worlds they ruled cannot be quite whole again.

If Armageddon were suddenly to overtake us, the scientists and social scientists of the future, while searching through the debris, would render a mixed verdict on American Jewish life in the mid-twentieth century. It is safe to say that they would rate highly the Jewish standard of living, its financial and social achievements, its contribution to medicine, law, science, entertainment, and government. But what would they have to say about the quality of Jewish life? How would they rate the stability of the Jewish family? How would they judge the Jewish contribution to things of the spirit? How would they assess the Jews' confidence in themselves and in their outlook on life in general and their purpose in the world of men? What would be their estimate of present-day Jewry's contribution to social justice, human equality, and universal morality? And, finally, how would they evaluate the voices Jews listen to these days and the objects to which they give their allegiance?

Dr. William Haber puts it aptly when he says: "We (the Jews) have assigned our heritage to the synagogue. Even while we won acceptance of the designation 'Jew,' we have made Judaism not a way of life but an episode on the calendar."[14] The American Jews have no problem of Americanization. They are Americans.[15] As a matter of fact, the problem is not of mere survival. Jews will survive as a group, and, despite the fact that many of them would like to fuse and disappear, they cannot, because the doors to the inner sanctum of oblivium are closed to them. Jews will continue to exist, but physical existence alone is hardly an admirable state of being. Their real problem is one of the psyche, the soul.[16] The most elementary student of human behavior is aware that, in the final analysis, one's ability to endure any conflict depends largely upon his orientation to something solid and well anchored and that, involved in this orientation, are three factors: his self-respect, his capacity to enjoy his existence, and his conviction as to the general purposefulness of his life. Confusion and anxiety develop when individuals lose their values and norms which deal with the desirable and with the expected way of behavior. Suffused with physical safety, mere digits in the great society, many Jews are becoming depressingly restless, spiritually hollow, and deeply skeptical about their personal worth in the scheme of things; they find themselves floundering about in a shadowy destiny—neither proud of their past nor proud of their future. They, of all people, recognize that denial of these facts, indulgence in fantasy, or seeking sedation in drugs, alcohol, or business are not true solutions but temporary escapes—thus they are becoming, as individuals, more and more disturbed under the veneer of sophistication and polish. They are still confronted with the traumatic dilemma: "To be or not to be a Jew."[17]

[14] William Haber, "You Have to Work at It," The *National Jewish Monthly*, LXXIX (September, 1964), 22.
[15] Will Herberg makes this abundantly clear in his essay on American religious sociology, *Protestant–Catholic–Jew* (Garden City: Anchor Books, 1960).
[16] Dr. O. Hobart Mowrer discusses this matter of "soulogy" in his deeply disturbing book, *The Crises in Psychiatry and Religion* (New York: Van Nostrand, 1961), 10.
[17] Mordecai M. Kaplan, *The Future of the American Jew* (New York: Mac-

Bernard Rosenberg and Gilbert Shapiro sum up most prophetically the American Jewish dilemma today: "While you can't go home again, there is little harm in reminiscing." So they reminisce with the following poignant observation: "We have moved from pogrom to personal slight, from exclusion at large to exclusion from the union club, and only the insensitive could deny that this represents real progress measurable in human blood. But one consequence of this change is a source of new suffering from a situation of relativity, certainty, and predictability in our dealing with people to one of total ambiguity."[18]

This does remain certain: such drastic overturnings of the traditional and the familiar, such swift breaks with the past, surely do not come from trivial causes. There are indeed many causes for this situation. The first and foremost is that, transplanted to America, the old Judaic philosophy of life soon discovered unforeseen obstacles in its path in the bittersweet collision of the worlds. The dream of the shtetl was gradually but surely being watered down.

The conflict between the two worlds proved to be a mixed blessing for the American Jews. On the one hand Jews recognize well their need for becoming more integrated into the host culture, while at the same time they are fully aware that if they break further with the past they will surely lose the formula whereby they survived for thousands of years. Many Jews today believe that the emancipation which they are experiencing in America will prove for them a flattering illusion, will break the Jews' belief in themselves and in their mission, and therewith their real will to exist as Jews. Naturally, they find this condition unpalatable and painful. At the moment, one of the consequences is that many of them are doing their utmost to become cul-

---

millan Co., 1948), 3. Rabbi Kaplan has long been concerned with the problem of the future of the American Jew. Rabbi Kaplan taught the writer while he was attending the Graduate School for Jewish Social Work in New York City in 1929–30, and he well recalls this courageous and dedicated man who understood so keenly the enormous challenge facing Judaism and the individual Jew in modern America.

[18] Rosenburg and Shapiro, "Marginality and Jewish Humor," 70.

turally more American, socially more Jewish, and theologically more Unitarian.[19]

Rabbi Morris Adler of Detroit, in answering the question "Will there be Jews in 2084?" begins by saying that this question "is born of a recognition that we are in the midst of a revolutionary, indeed, cataclysmic period. Institutions, ideas, practices, and traditions long revered and maintained have crumbled and fallen into the dustbin of history. In an age so irreverent and iconoclastic where the past is concerned, will the Jewish group, despite its long unbroken existence, succeed in surviving? In truth there has been a breakdown of considerable proportions of Jewish disciplines and practices. Jewish knowledge, which was once widespread and universally respected is now the possession of only a few. One looks at one's children and grandchildren and wonders what kind of Jews they will be, indeed if they will be Jews at all."[20]

Rabbi Adler does present a "positive dimension" to the question, that despite all the negative aspects of this condition "the modern Jew has resolved to remain within the fold. It seems to be a resolve that will endure. To be sure, this determination has not yet gone much further than organizational affiliation, inducing a prosperity in the membership of our synagogues and temples. Perhaps the critics are right: it is superficial and indecisive."[21]

Dr. Louis Kaplan, president of the Baltimore Hebrew College, be-

---

[19] The authors of the analytical study evaluating the characteristics of contemporary Jewish life in America, *Children of the Gilded Ghetto*, have this to add regarding the impact of the host culture on the Jewish group: "The Jewish community like all minority communities, has been transformed in response to the changing social tensions of the minority situation." Judith R. Kramer and Seymour Leventman, *Children of the Gilded Ghetto* (New Haven: Yale University Press, 1961), 4.

It is interesting to note at this point that whereas Irish Catholics and German Lutherans also became Americanized they remained Catholics and Lutherans, but Jews became so American that they would convert their Judaism into just another set of beliefs which would make them no different from anyone else. Why Jews want to be like everyone else is hard to understand when one realizes that what is really worth preserving in their lives are their differences.

[20] Morris Adler, "Will There Be Jews in 2084?", *National Jewish Monthly*, LXXVIII (March, 1964), 14.

[21] *Ibid.*, 14.

lieves that this trend is superficial and indecisive. He says: "To assume that a greater identification with the synagogue and/or that the establishment of the centrality of the synagogue will raise the level of Jewish life, is unrealistic."[22] From the midst of all the dramatic transformation in American Jewish life has come the realization that the mills of time have caught up with the modern American Jews and that today, in the vernacular of the academy, they may be said to be living at the same time in a spiritual kindergarten and a materialistic graduate school.

For untold ages Jews have found their religion the home to which they may always go. Today they lack this feeling of home. This is truly one of the most distinguishing things about Jewish life in America today. Spiritually there is no place to go. There are thousands, even millions, of people who are "Jews" but for whom the synagogue seems to be hollow on the inside and all facade on the outside. In the shtetl the synagogue belonged to the Jews, in American Jews belong to the synagogue; in the shtetl there was a "we" feeling in connection with the synagogue, in America it is the "they" feeling which makes itself felt. In the shtetl synagogue everyone knew that much depended upon him, on his time, talent, energy, faith, strength, and courage; today in America the synagogue is well organized and well attended, and gives the impression that it does not need help, only money to run the machine. The result of this outlook has been much scorn for the spiritual aspects of Judaism and much cynicism against all idealism.

Perhaps the American Jewish outlook merely reflects Rabbi Abraham Heschel's observation regarding contemporary man in general: "I maintain that the agony of contemporary man is the agony of spiritually stunted man, that the image of man is larger than the frame into which he has been contracted. . . . The grandeur and uniqueness of man is his ability to realize that God has a stake in his existence. . . . There is only one way to define the Jewish re-

[22] Louis Kaplan, *National Jewish Monthly*, LXXVIII (March, 1964), 15.

ligion—as the awareness of God's interest in man, of a covenant between God and man."[23]

In truth, what place has the synagogue in American Jewish life? It is a fact that there has been an amazing growth of synagogue membership in the last twenty years, although attendance is something else. C. Bezalel Sherman says in this connection that "there is no evidence that the increase in synagogue membership and in Jewish school enrollment has brought with it a correspondingly increased piety. On the contrary there is every indication that American Jews are becoming more lax in their religious practices."[24]

We hear all around us of a turning back to Judaism and to more creative interest. Yet before we get overly excited about this salutary development we must be cautioned: when religion is handled by the yard and wrapped in cellophane, when religious activity is sold like tons of bricks and steel, with spontaneous inspiration left out, then all we have is secularism triumphing again, this time in the name of Judaism.

On Friday evenings when Jewish congregations and rabbis all over America enter their synagogues there is an air of expectancy that something special may happen—but what does happen? Do the congregants really know why they are there? Do they know what they are seeking? Who is in that synagogue with them? Or is the whole business merely habit?

Most modern American synagogues have revolted against the religiosity of the shtetl (it must be admitted that they cannot turn back the clock to the shtetl time) and have fervently embraced the social sciences, literature, and mass entertainment (note the grand and exorbitant wedding and Bar Mitzvah affairs) and like Mephistopheles with Dr. Faustus have offered their followers an abundance of "wealth." They have manicured their sacred humanistic and spiritual values into mere fashionable fads which can destroy their age-old ideals and values more surely than the Nazi barbarians. In gen-

[23] Abraham Joshua Heschel, "A Visit with Rabbi Heschel," *Think*, XXX (Jan.-Feb., 1964), 16–18.
[24] Sherman, *The Jew Within American Society*, 221.

eral, the American rabbi no longer speaks for his followers, for the home, for Judaism; he speaks for the synagogue. He wants to be popular, he wants to attract not only members of his congregation but also non-Jews to his lectures. He wants to be accepted by the crowd, he wants to adjust to "the vanities and vulgarities of the day." An extreme example of this is the rabbi in Mississippi who told a business and professional women's club that "what America needs is more Mississippi not less" (the Memphis *Commercial Appeal*, October 24, 1962). This rabbi should take a lesson from Pastor Martin Niemöller of Germany, who explained his tragic experience with this statement: *I didn't speak up.* "In Germany they came for the Communists and I didn't speak up because I wasn't a Communist. Then they came for the Jews, and I didn't speak up because I wasn't a Jew. Then they came for the trade unionists, and I didn't speak up because I wasn't a trade unionist. Then they came for the Catholics and I didn't speak up because I was a Protestant. Then they came for me—and by that time no one was left to speak up."

Many of the modern-day rabbis would promote Judaism by bringing tired business men and women into a synagogue to attend a service whose appeal rests on the twin virtues of brevity and the absence of theological and socially liberal preaching, which is precisely what their congregations want. The writer's own congregation was recently in the throes of obtaining a rabbi. As a member of the committee whose job it was to choose the proper person, he had the opportunity to discuss the necessary qualifications with many members of the congregation. In general, what we wanted was a rabbi six feet tall, with blond hair, blue eyes, and a Yale accent—one who would be acceptable to the community at large, one who would leave "this race relations business" alone, and who would enhance the image of the Jewish congregation. (It is interesting to note that we hired a rabbi who is not six feet tall, who does not have blue eyes, blond hair, nor a Yale accent, but who is, nevertheless, a brilliant biblical scholar and who has already enhanced the image of the Jewish congregation in this community.)

This is a sad commentary on a large portion of American Jewish life and its leadership. Once upon a time Jews believed that their religion was destined to lead a bewildered mankind out of the wilderness into a promised land, but along the way, with many of its Christian neighbors, it seems to have lost direction. The question "Can the blind lead the blind?" may well be pointed at present-day Judaism.

So what are many Jews in America doing about all this? First, they shield their troubled hearts, confused minds, and sickened souls behind ingenious masks of milk-toast optimism, then they make sacrifices to hospitals, schools, playgrounds, and museums, forgetting that the Talmud describes the Almighty as saying to Israel: "Think not that in offering sacrifices ye are doing my pleasure, ye are doing your own"; and, finally, with a hope and a prayer, they dream that some miracle will come along to save them, that a messiah of some sort will arrive suddenly and all will be well with them.

There is a talmudic legend which is most timely at this crucial period in the life of American Jewry. This legend relates that a rabbi, one day, met Elijah the Prophet and asked him when the Messiah would come. "Go," replied Elijah, "and ask the Messiah himself. You will find him mingling with the poor and the oppressed. A man of sorrow himself, he cares for those who suffer and binds up their wounds." The rabbi found the Messiah and asked him when he would come. His answer was, "Today." In short, the Messiah is always with us if only we grasp the meaning of what is meant by God and His messenger to us.

A symphony comes to an end when its themes have all been developed and worked through to their conclusion; a dream comes to an end similarly when the questions which it has asked have been dealt with and some answer has been found. But the Old Testament does not end in any such way. Its questions have been stated but not answered. There has been the promise that they will be answered by the Lord's future action, but the promise has not been fulfilled. The Messianic hope remains an unfulfilled hope; men are left waiting for a future event.[25] Jews in America are waiting for such an event.

[25] Hebert, *The Old Testament from Within*, 123.

There are two roads which may be taken by Jews in their efforts to reach this "event." One is implied in the prophetic statement by Rabbi Eisendrath:

And it came to pass after many millennia that the descendants of Abraham fled from the lash of many nations and came at last to the golden land of a New Jerusalem and it was a place known as America. . . . And it came to pass, in the latter part of the twentieth century, that Jews ceased to remember their past and their distinctive ways and they became like everybody else—and often more so. . . . And so it is written that, in the golden land of the New Jerusalem, amidst freedom and plenty and the warm bonds of brotherhood, Judaism died painlessly in its sleep. And there was no rending of garments, no heaping of ashes and the voice of the Kaddish was not heard in the land.[26]

Obviously this road is both spiritually arid and socially unlovely.

The other road implies a long and serious look into the "mirror," and an honest recognition that there is a direct and unseverable relationship between "Jewishness" and survival, between the attitude held by Jews about themselves and Judaism and about the future of Jewry. And, finally, the other road involves a realization that the value of studying the Torah, the Talmud, the Wisdom of the Fathers, as well as the appreciation of art, poetry, and music are seldom precisely measurable in terms of goods produced, or man-hours saved, or an increase in personal income.

Anyone who has some sensitivity regarding the source and nature of the fearful anxieties of our times must realize that, sooner or later, the majority of Jews in America today are destined to experience the profound sickness of the soul which comes with a dawning awareness of the deep loss of spiritual orientation. In describing the burdens of man in general, Will Herberg has portrayed graphically the burden of the American Jew: "He has drained the universe of value and thus deprived himself of all possibility of finding a secure anchorage in reality for the ideas and purposes that constitute significant human life. . . . In short, modern man no longer possesses any unity or

[26] Eisendrath, *Can Faith Survive?*, 10. Used by permission of McGraw Hill Book Company.

orientation in life. He stands lost, bewildered, unable to understand himself or to master the forces of his inner and outer life."[27] The crisis of such serious illness is one of the rare moments when the role of religion becomes sharply focused. A person in such circumstances can often realize with dizzy suddenness that life is a swiftly passing experience. It can even lead one to a re-examination of the way he has been living his life and to a reconsideration of how he ought to live it in order to give meaning to his existence. In the case the modern American Jew it may be that at this point he can find in Judaism the warm, secure chimney corner of old, the power to hear again the echo of its own wonder, the drive to perpetuate the image of Moses, the authority to unlock again the secrets of Avrom, the urge to rediscover God, and the spark which can breed dignified men and women admirably equipped to stand up among all people, everywhere.

But the picture is not entirely bleak—there are signs that a new generation, neither molded originally by the shtetl tradition nor scarred by the swift changes in American life, is emerging. Rabbi Morris Adler paints the picture admirably without disgust or enchantment when he says: "As I study the Jewish outlook it seems to be characterized by two attitudes: realism and optimism. We are not blind to some of the grim facts about American Jewish life, its superficiality, the lack of translation of Jewish values into personal life. We are not fooled by the numbers and the large meetings. We recognize the cultural poverty of so many of our programs. But on the other hand, to use a Biblical phrase, we are prisoners of hope."[28]

Whatever be the pros and the cons of the situation within American Jewry today, one fact remains. This generation of Jews cannot deny that there is an incongruity within their ranks, and that the reason for their dread and restlessness and lack of inwardness is that a high degree of disintegration exists both within themselves as individuals, within their component dimensions, and between them

[27] Will Herberg, *Judaism and Modern Man* (New York: Meridian Books, 1959), 25.
[28] Adler, "Will There Be Jews in 2084?", 22.

and the larger community. Modern American Jews must realize further that, whereas they might want to substitute for a living and vital Judaism a new system which would indeed emancipate them from the basic Jewish style of living, this can no more be done than substituting a diet of water for food and then expecting the constitution to survive. It is impossible to believe that Jews can continue to exist without those presuppositions which have given them identity for four thousand years. Obviously a renaissance in American Jewish life is necessary which will enable Jews to advance from the uncertain atmosphere in which they find themselves, to a new and higher plane. Moralistic exhortations and individual effort, however sincere, will not suffice. The matter has to be treated as a serious social problem in Jewish life, it needs to be recognized, analyzed, planned for, and solutions suggested.

A hint of the solution may be found in Isaiah (58:7): "deal thy bread to the hungry and that thou bring the poor that are cast out to thy house. . . ." It is the contention of the writer that a return to and an emphasis upon the Jewish family might well help generate another revolution in Jewish life, bringing with it a new age of Jewish asceticism, stability, vigor, and moralistic tone, as well as a brightened spiritual quality, and the replacement with a new (not with the old), a special type of Judaism. A hard look at the contemporary scene in America indicates that the role of the family in American Jewish life must become increasingly important as the other institutions seem to lose the strength, authority, and substance to influence Jewish life. For many, many generations has the Jewish family been dramatically successful in holding the family together and in inculcating the ideals of Judaism into the very heart and soul of its members. In spite of crushing disasters and demoralizing oppressions, the Jewish family has never quite lost its hold on virtue, faith, and hope. Throughout the millennia clarity of membership in the Jewish family has helped insure continuity not only in the life of the group but in the life of the individual. The Jewish family has always had and can have again a way of life contagious among those who are part of it, drawing them together in a mysterious dynamism and generating a sense of spiritual commitment and a vision beyond comprehension. It may be the one agent which can teach Jews what it is they must do and what it is they must become in the short space between birth and death.

In short, it may be that a revitalized American Jewish family can supply answers that are not being found elsewhere. The new American family, if it could speak, might say to all American Jews everywhere, in the words of Jeremiah (24:6): "I will set mine eyes upon them for good . . . I will build them, and not pull them down; I will plant them, and not pluck them up."

VIII

Thou Shalt Raise Up the Foundations of Generations

Chaucer wrote that "life is a thinne subtil knitting of things." This simple observation describes accurately the structure and function of the Jewish family system throughout the ages. It was this knitting of things which was the subtle yet powerful element in the rearing of children, and the influences it exerted in determining the form and scope of Jewish life that account, in large part, for its survival. It unlocked a consciousness which originated in some remote time and place but became immediate in the shtetl atmosphere, and cast a shadow reaching across to the shores of America.

No matter the pros and cons of the Jewish "problem" in America today, all will agree that in this environment a new type of Jewish family is emerging—a fact which nags painfully at most American Jews. They find themselves imprisoned in a world of contingency. They are in the center of the great move toward secularism; they have become part of the overwhelming ferment which has acquired universal proportions and which is sweeping them along with all the rest of Americana. The impact of the social changes around them and the problems crowding in upon them from all sides are further complicated by deep emotional strains resulting from the feeling of being a minority group, of being eternal strangers wherever they go. Jews today in America are, in a sense, hypnotized by their social environment, and they cannot tell where lies the dividing line between what they are and what their society is—a society which is changing so rapidly that no one can really keep up with it or tie himself to it. Thus it is that the American Jew finds himself wavering between his ethnic folkways and the mores of the host society and feels the subtle conflict from the pressures. Say what we will, to the Gentile he is not an American Jew but a Jew living in America.

The prophetic words of Amos (8:11, 12) keep creeping into his subconscious: "Behold, the days come, saith the Lord God, that I will send famine in the land, not a famine of bread, nor a thirst for water, but of hearing the words of the Lord; and they shall wander from sea to sea, and from the north even to the east, they shall run to and fro to seek the word of the Lord, and shall not find it."

When American Jews begin thinking about this situation calmly and soberly they will feel a kind of panic, for no matter whether they belong to the synagogue or not, whether they belong and go only once a year, whether they spend the high holy days at Grossingers or in Miami, whether they take their virtues and tastes like their shirts and furniture from the marketplace, there are moments when some inexplicable thing touches their sensitive nerve of nostalgia and memories long hidden in the corners of their hearts suddenly explode and splinter their souls. Deep down in the silence of their beings they somehow realize that they are now living on the rapidly shrinking psychic income from the capital investment of Jews of the last two thousand years and that, labor as they may, as long as they live in a Gentile nation-state they must always sit near the door where they inevitably arouse distrust.[1] Say what they will, do what they will, go where they will, think what they will, the truism ever remains: "Being a Jew does have consequences for one's behavior. . . ." The Jew is distinguished from all other people by certain characteristics and no matter how unstable these may be, no matter how much he wishes to be like everybody else, he will have to realize that the

[1] George Steiner, "A Kind of Survivor," *Commentary*, XXXIX (February, 1965), 37.

visible reality hides a deeper one and that ultimately all his actions, achievements, goals, and dreams must rest on things unseen.

This may indeed be a very high psychic price to pay merely to discover the answer to Job's question: "Who am I?" In the interim the American Jews' longing for a real identity remains unfulfilled. And people at the crossroad of history sometimes do stop and ask why. Thus many are the lessons which Jews may learn about their present life and their future destiny in America by a vehement and biting questioning of the revolution which is taking place in the American Jewish family today.

Outstanding students of the family have concluded that the modern basic family has two basic functions: to train children in the way of group culture and to provide psychic security for adults.[2] In the case of the Jewish family must be added another basic function: to generate what is termed "Jewishness" which is so essential in the matter of survival. It has ever been the ideal among Jews that, through the family, children were brought into this world and reared "that a man's house might not die out in Israel."

The basic features of the American Jewish family have their roots in the past, during which time Jews have been able to achieve the ideals of their family through a special pattern of socialization sternly inculcated into their children. The essential characteristics of this pattern were pride in Judaism, concern over things of the spirit, emphasis upon learning, respect for the aged, avoidance of boasting and gluttony, implicit obedience, responsibility of parents and grandparents, respect for women and the commandment "Honor thy father and thy mother." And the result? The result was a people who were spiritually tough, persistent in their intention, demanding in their purpose, affectionate in their relationship to each other, and fanatically

---

[2] Our concern here is not with theoretical changes now occurring in the family per se nor with the influences such changes may or may not have on society in general but with the more complicated picture of the revolution in the American Jewish family and its particular influence on Judaism itself and on the survival of Jewry. As a matter of fact, the American Jewish family is still considered one of the most stable of all groups, and its struggle for survival is vigorous.

loyal to their God. Not only did this type of family system aid Jews to survive against great odds, but, without guns and swords, without bombs and armored divisions, Judaism made history; in fact, it has been considered by many as one of the great civilizing influences of all times.

A sobering awareness of the trend in Jewish life, then, indicates that one of the central problems facing American Jewry has to do with its family and its changing structure and function. In short, the present-day American Jewish family seems to have stored its noble ideals in mothballs and is going the way of all flesh. In part, at least, the degeneration in the American Jewish family is the result of forces in the wider cultural scene: conflicting role expectations in marriage, discontinuity in the training process of children, emphasis on romantic irresponsibility in the courtship techniques, decline in useful functions performed by children in the home or out, lack of religious activities in the home, emphasis upon youth, speed, and material success, and the stress on enjoyment and consumption as against work and study. In addition, there has been an estrangement from traditional values of Jewish life, a stifling of the Jewish self-consciousness, and the general lack of identification with the broader aspects of Judaism. It would appear that lastingness, stability, and tradition are being sacrificed to abundance, secularism, and to immediate pleasure.[3]

The Jewish family has become too scared of its children, the Jewish children too insecure in their remoteness from their parents, and the synagogue too much of a social organization for the good of the family or the synagogue or Judaism in general. Indeed, the Jews of America have outdone the Protestants in regard to the "Protestant ethic."

The young American Jew can change his name and address; he can change his religion, his country club, and perhaps become a hero, but the tragedy is that he will never be a Jewish hero. He no longer

[3] The problem is not one found only in America. The World Union of Jewish Students held a seminar at Egmond Aan Zee in Holland from December 29, 1963, to January 5, 1964. The theme of the congress was "Crisis in Jewry." "Crisis in Jewry," *Higher Education and Research in the Netherlands*, VIII, No. 2 (1964), p. 28.

feels the dignity of his grandfather; he no longer experiences the grandeur nor realizes the importance of his life as did his grandfather. As a matter of fact he often feels embarrassed in this new environment, like a Salvation Army lassie who might stray into a Roman Catholic church.[4]

There can be little question that there is a crisis in the American Jewish family which is having a sharp and telling impact upon American Jewry and which is demonstrating clearly the grey premonitions of the future.

It will be said that Jews throughout the ages have been a people beset with crises. This is true. However, the crisis faced by the American Jewish family is different in one major respect—it is mostly of Jewry's own making.

The American Jew is indeed a paradox. On the one hand he has an amazing heritage which goes back to the Haran desert where he found God, and yet today he stands in free, bountiful America, a stranger to himself.

Anatomically and neurologically he is no different from Moses, Rambam, Spinoza, or Tevye. He may be a little taller; he eats more meat and drinks more milk; he may be a little fairer of skin, and his nose may be less armenoid in structure (miscegenation will do that). What, then, is the difference? It is the way he looks at things and at himself that makes the difference. It has to do with his "cultural lenses." The answer is that in Babylon, in Toledo, and in "Kasrilevka" he described the facts of his behavior, experiences, and value system in terms of the concepts of the Torah, whereas in "Middleburg," U.S.A., he describes them in terms of what he reads in the Middleburg *Daily News*. The Jews of America with their fluorescent lights have come a long way from their co-religionists in the shtetl with their kerosene lamps, but the real question is not so much what sort of lights they have but what it is they read by these lights.

---

[4] The writer has expressed often to his non-Jewish friends in the community where he and his family have lived for a quarter of a century that, whereas most of the year he feels very much at home, there are several days when he feels frightfully alone—Christmas, Easter Sunday, and, particularly, Good Friday.

It is a common observation that man sees two ways, with his physical eye and with his "insight." The American Jew can turn his physical eye on the scene and observe that each generation in America seems to have children less Jewish than itself, and grandchildren still less; and he can turn on his other eyes in the direction of Isaiah (58:12) and become aware of a new judgment, a new commitment, and a new identification. Isaiah has been reminding Jews for ages that the places which have been desolated will be built up in them; that they will raise up the foundations of the generations to come and that they will be called the repairers of fences, turning the pathways into places of rest.

What is the path which can turn into rest? What are the foundations of generations and what are the fences which need repairing? Obviously, the path does not lead to the shtetl life, but by the same token neither does it lead into a dry, thirsty land of spiritual and social oblivion. For the foundations of generations we are driven to look back at a deeper level to the origin and nature of the Judaic ideals. Hard as it is to lay hold of these secrets of Jewry's endurance, resolution, and heroism, they are there even as the hills are there, albeit it is difficult to see hills while flying at thirty thousand feet in a jet going six hundred miles an hour.

The fences which need repairing have to do with "Jewishness." From early days the struggle for survival, both spiritual and cultural, has been demanded of Jews, and the struggle developed within this group the capacity to generate its own special style of living.[5]   At the present time Jews are fleeing from this style of living but they do not know where. They doubt a great many things about this style with a kind of doubt, however, which "the heart does not share with the mind or tongue."

To be sure, the final destination of the Jewish voyage lies beyond the horizon, yet all will agree that there is a tangible feeling within the ranks of Jewry that something important is at hand which calls

[5] Modern Jews have forgotten that their forefathers were considered as a people out of step not because they refused to comply but, perhaps, because, in the words of Thoreau, they were listening to another drummer.

for the opening of a new dialogue somewhere between apathy and panic regarding the fundamental requirements of Jewish survival. This remains certain: the situation as it stands now definitely forms no reason for excessive optimism or simplism regarding the pressing issues confronting Jewry and Judaism.

The rabbi is no longer the voice of the people, as his ideas seem to be falling on soil not prepared for germination. Once upon a time it was the synagogue which housed much of the accumulated wisdom of Judaism gathered through the centuries of experience, and which cared for it, classified it, reinterpreted it, and projected it to its followers. This is no longer true because far too many Jews today have lost the taste for Torah and prayer and, at best, merely spout pious platitudes without getting their feet near those mountains about which Isaiah speaks when he says, "How beautiful upon the mountains are the feet of him that bringeth good tidings and publisheth peace."

In the light of these sociopsychological facts it becomes evident that the American Jew is now confronting himself with the compelling need to create a new identification for himself, for only in this way can the threat to his survival be checked.[6]

It is the conviction of this writer that what is desperately needed today is a critical "minding" of the American Jewish family and, on the basis of this minding, a systematic and dynamic analysis of the structure and function of this particular family system with the hope that its strength and weaknesses may be discovered. This is no longer a matter of judgment but a matter of serious and honest evaluation. Perhaps a return to the wise dicta of the Fathers: *Taharas ha mishpochah*—to be concerned with the purity of the family, and *Peru oov'voo*—to have children and rear them properly, could release a creative energy among these people which would bring them a new

[6] One may or may not agree with Arthur Koestler's outlook on Jews and Judaism; however, the man has obviously done some serious thinking regarding this particular social phenomenon. His following observation calls for special attention. "Up to now the Jews' fate lay in the hands of the Gentiles. At present it lies entirely in their own hands. The wandering Jew has arrived at a crossroads and the consequences of his present choice will make themselves felt for centuries." Koestler, *The Trail of the Dinosaur*, 106.

wholeness, a new religious depth, a new dedication and dimension to their understanding of self as an individual and as a member of the Jewish group, and the answer to their spiritual quest for an all-inclusive *Weltanschauung* (world view), as well as a fullness of personal well-being.

Among the behavioral sciences today there is a virtual consensus of the concept discovered ages ago by the Jews, mainly that the relationship between children and parents is the basic determinant of the personality of the individual; that the unique companionship, intellectual, emotional, spiritual, found in this environment—the companionship between thee and me—generates the stimulation and interchange of ingredients which emphasize man's proud, yet sometimes tragic consciousness of human values which have to do with that imponderable thing we call immortality.

Anyone who questions the special sensitivity of the role to be played by the Jewish family in the existence, stability, and even survival of the Jewish group should note the startling statement in the *National Jewish Monthly* of May, 1965: "A man calling himself Rabbi Sherwin T. Wine, who serves an institution calling itself a synagogue in Detroit, declared recently from a rostrum he designates as a pulpit that he does not believe in God."[7] This is not as bizarre as it may appear at first glance. In the midst of a boastful materialism shot through with greed and hypocrisy, the magic of sincerity, the importance of dignity, and the emphasis upon spiritual values are subject to ridicule if not worse. It often happens that individuals as well as groups become so preoccupied with their material mansions that they are inclined to forget the foundations of those mansions. But then it is difficult to build solid foundations for such mansions when, as it is written in Genesis, "and slime had they for mortar."

One might properly ask at this point what effect that event in Detroit—although it is only a footnote in American Jewish history—will have on the already confused Jewish youth, on their judgment,

---

[7] This situation, one might add without fear of contradiction, is the *piece de resistance* of absurdity in the case of the Vanishing Jew. Here is a rabbi who can, in all sincerity, say: "I am an atheist, thank God!"

courage, dedication, and their willingness to suffer for the future. What will it do to their already well-worn group fabric of spiritual experience and to their entire bundle of Hebraic heritage? Nothing too devastating, probably, except add to their apathy and panic, subtle as they may be. It will hardly encourage the Jew to turn the world upside down as did Isaiah, or to increase his zeal to save his synagogue or his family from extinction. Chances are it will encourage him, rather, to compete more strenuously for the "young man of the year" award from the Junior Chamber of Commerce and to make greater effort to get into the nearby country club.

In regard to the frantic search for security Helen Keller has a profound observation to make: "Security is mostly a superstition. It does not exist in nature, nor do the children of men as a whole experience it. Avoiding danger is no safer in the long run than outright exposure. The fearful are caught as often as the bold. Faith alone defends."

The Nazis believed they could destroy Jewry by burning books and synagogues and by intoxicating their own "brown shirts" with vitriolic hatred. All the American Jews need to do to destroy themselves is to leave their books unread, their synagogues unattended, and become intoxicated by drinking "new Wine from new bottles."

Members of Rabbi Wine's congregation must be asking themselves at least one pertinent question these days. Since each Jew owes his existence as a Jew to the fact that God has always made demands upon him, who will now make the demands upon them so that they may remain Jews? Who knows? Perhaps Nietszche was right when he said that God is dead, that we have slain Him.

No matter what one feels about Rabbi Wine's outlook, this must be said in his favor. His attitude about God reflects the attitude found among many, many American Jews, and there is an unmistakable ring of truth in this reflection which will not easily fade away. If this trend should gather momentum then Arnold Toynbee's prediction will surely prove to be correct: the modern Jew will become a fossil, a physical remnant of a society which is extinct, and Jews will never be able to boast of tomorrow.

Thus it is that, increasingly in the last twenty-five years, Judaism in America has moved into a critical period in which it is re-examining and appraising its structures, its functions, and its goals. Not the least important of these issues is the place of the Jewish family in the overall scheme of things.

All human life is essentially dramatic, and in no other setting may be found such intense drama as in the family relationship. Here is an example of a truly transcendent phenomenon, and herein lies the attraction and magic of the family. The family is the first institution that greets us when we enter the world, and its function is to teach us how to face this world and its problems and how to solve them— in short, how to measure our strength against it. For many generations the Jewish family held on to those presupposing and calming influences which directed the lives of its members, generating in them a drive and passion, an internal churning and inspiration which promised things in the future, among these being a mind that understands and creates, a spirit that suffers and sacrifices, a heart that loves and is at peace with itself. Today in America too many Jewish families do not possess the space, time, nor motivation to convert their traditional riches into a meaningful and satisfying articulate expression of life that could aid their members in the search for a self-recognition of their worth and their honor which might enable them to face the hour and the turmoil it has brought them. Rather has the family helped to alienate them further from the certainties of their forefathers. Man is by nature a stranger to the world, and he desperately needs to belong to something. Alienation is one of the major problems of American Jews, and it can be a very dark and painful experience.

As Milton Gordon says: "Frustrated and not fully accepted by the broader social world he [the Jew] wishes to enter, ambivalent in his attitude toward the more restricted social world to which he has ancestral rights, and beset by conflicting cultural standards, he develops, according to the classic conception, personality traits of insecurity, moodiness, hypersensitivity, excessive self-consciousness and nervous strain."[8] Indeed, this exaggerated idea of going it alone, of independence from family, from group, from God has brought especially heavy burdens to the American Jewish shoulders. The doctrine of depending on nothing but himself and on things, the philosophy of "I and it," rather than "I and thee" and "I and thou," has brought a sadness one sees only on the face of the saddest clown in the circus. Jews in America must learn quickly that without "depending" on lasting objects there will soon be left no individual Jew, no Jewish family, no Jewish group, and no Judaism.

There are many complex and dynamic reasons for this condition but the most important one, as the writer has said before, seems to be the passionate desire on the part of American Jews to conform to those about them. However, according to Norman Bentwitch, the tragedy is that "the more desperately they argued that they were the same, the more vividly the differences stood out; indeed the anxiety to deny the differences was itself a barrier to its disappearance. . . ."[9] One can well understand and appreciate the subtle as well as the bold, the overt as well as the covert ideological forces which are impinging upon American Jews and their families from all sides, but it does not necessarily mean that they need to destroy the age-old adherence to many of their traditional ideals. Ruth N. Anshen, an outstanding student of family life speaks of the emotional intensity of the conflict between the faith of the immigrant parents and their children and of its drastic effects upon them. But she adds that it does not follow that this condition is inevitable: "Many an orthodox Jewish home, and many an Italian Catholic or German Lutheran family have held fast to the faith of their fathers without compromising the faith which has symbolized and secured the unity of the family."[10]

[8] Milton M. Gordon, *Assimilation in American Life* (New York: Oxford University Press, 1964), 57. It may be added that, because of this condition, Jews are also inclined to develop such characteristics as greater insight, motivation, and creativity.

[9] Norman Bentwitch, *The Jew in Our Time* (Baltimore: Penguin Books, 1960), 92.

[10] Ruth N. Anshen (ed.), *The Family: Its Function and Destiny* (New York: Harper and Brothers, 1959), 317.

Indeed, American Jews must be reminded at this point that no institution, be it governmental, economic, or familial, can last very long without a vision and a *raison d'etre* which lights its way in history and guides it along that way in times of crises, be they crises of extreme success or of extreme failure.

There is a painful stubbornness inherent in the problem of the American Jewish family, for, despite the many strictures within its framework and the many shortcomings within its functional operations, there is a certain excellence within that family system, and it possesses many positive elements when compared to the families of other ethnic and religious groups. This becomes a very important sociopsychological fact since the paramount thesis in this entire undertaking is that in the case of Jews, at any rate, there is no institution which can replace the family in providing the mechanism for handling the motivational problems of personality adjustment. The Jewish family has ever had to do more than merely perform the basic functions in relation to children. As a matter of fact, among Jews, the family has been more than a sociological complex, it has actually been a therapeutic institution.[11]

Many studies covering contemporary American society indicate that the Jewish family is one of the most stable of all groups. In a study made in Detroit it was found that Jewish families had the lowest divorce rate of all religious groups including the Catholics.[12] Monahan and Kephart in their survey "Divorce and Desertion by Religious

[11] Dr. Nathaniel S. Lehrman makes an interesting observation regarding Jewish mental health. There are more Jews in the field of psychiatry both as physicians and as patients than members of any other group. Dr. Lehrman explains the reasons for this phenomenon: "At least two important factors can be isolated for the larger number of Jewish psychotherapists. One is negative: the relative lack of prejudice in the field; the other is positive: the hope that psychotherapy can cure the aching souls of our time. . . . Believing that psychotherapy *does* have answers, Jews have also tended much more to consider as 'sick' the ordinary problems of living which their non-Jewish neighbors accept as 'normal.' Hence, the Jew seems to have become rather more prone than his Gentile neighbor to seek psychotherapeutic assistance for any given level of 'uneasiness.' " Nathaniel S. Lehrman, "Jews and Psychiatry," *American Judaism*, XIV (Summer, 1965), 6–7.

[12] Derek L. Phillips (ed.), *Studies in American Society* (New York: Thomas Y. Crowell Co., 1960), 13.

and Mixed Groups," discovered that Jewish families break up less than non-Jewish ones.[13] Meyer Nimkoff found in his studies that the average age of marriage in the United States is highest for Jews. Rabbi Eisendrath tells us that one of the particular characteristics of the American Jewish family is the relatively low birth rate. Jews are probably America's most efficient practitioners of family planning. They no doubt have among the smallest families, if not the smallest, among all groups.[14]

Furthermore, the proportions of the Jewish population for high school and college are somewhat higher than in the general population. Jews "graduate from college at about three times the rate of non-Jews and data on labor force characteristics indicate that in cities outside New York and other large population centers, Jews tend to congregate in the proprietorship, managerial, professional and clerical occupations."[15]

Finally and equally important is the fact that interfaith marriage, which can prove to be such a seriously disruptive element within a religious group, is still the lowest for Jews among the religious denominations in America. Despite the relatively small percentage the number is large enough to cause concern. Interfaith marriage between Jews and non-Jews places added stress and strains upon an institution which is at this moment already going through difficult and trying changes.

Rabbi Louis Finkelstein explains well the importance of conversion of the non-Jew in the case of interfaith marriage. "Because of the special place the home occupies in Judaism as a center of religious life and worship . . . Judaism holds it essential that both parties to a Jewish marriage be members of the Jewish faith . . . it is not pos-

---

[13] Thomas P. Monahan and William M. Kephart, "Divorce and Desertion by Religious and Mixed Groups," *American Journal of Sociology*, LIX (March, 1954), 454–60.

[14] Paul C. Glick, "Intermarriage and Fertility Patterns Among Persons in Major Religious Groups," *Eugenics Quarterly*, VII (March, 1960), 31–38.

[15] Morris Fine and Milton Himmelfarb (eds.), *American Jewish Yearbook, 1963* (Philadelphia: Jewish Publication Society of America, 1963), 64.

sible for the home to function in the manner prescribed by Jewish law unless both husband and wife are of the Jewish faith."[16]

The overall rate of interfaith marriage among Jews is about 7 percent; however, studies of this phase of Jewish life have indicated that as the size of the Jewish community decreases the level of intermarriage is likely to increase. A survey covering interfaith marriage of Jews in America indicates that in Washington, D.C. (180,000 Jews) the rate was 13.1 percent; in cities of 10,000 or more the rate was 34.2 percent, and it was almost twice as high in towns and rural areas.[17]

The effect of interfaith marriage upon children is noted in the *American Jewish Yearbook* for 1963:

> That intermarriage usually spells the end of belonging to the Jewish group is demonstrated by the fact that in at least 70 per cent of the mixed families in Greater Washington the children were not identified with the Jewish group. . . . In the absence of large-scale immigration, it may well be that intermarriage is going to be of ever increasing significance in the future demographic balance of the Jewish population in the United States.[18]

Children have always been masterpieces in the making, and for a long time Jews were experts at this delicate and rewarding art. In fact, Jewry's future has in the past belonged first to God and then to its children. So it is an ironic twist that never before have Jewish children played so important a role in Jewish life as they do today, particularly since in their flight toward the secularization of their way of life Jews find that God is becoming less and less essential as a source of strength and direction.

It is, of course, very difficult to make any but general statements

---

[16] Louis Finkelstein (ed.), *The Jews* (New York: Harper and Row, 1950), II, 1329.

[17] An extreme example of this is the Louisiana community studied by the author in 1950 where he found that among the Jewish group of that generation about 90 percent had married out of the faith, and that in every case their offspring were reared in the Christian church. Benjamin Kaplan, *The Eternal Stranger* (New York: Bookman, 1957), 99.

[18] Fine and Himmelfarb, *American Jewish Yearbook, 1963*, p. 53.

regarding specific characteristics of Jewish children, albeit there have been some very reliable studies made of Jewish children, their attitudes, values, orientations, and goals in life. It is important to note that Jewish children of today have, by and large, made a decisive break with what they considered the environmental image of the past. The old sense of uniqueness and the special Hebraic destiny which their grandparents and even parents had seems to be fading.

The typical Jewish child of today wants to feel that he belongs to the middle class in the American social structure, that he is like everybody else, and that his Jewishness is no different from Christianity. He wants his life to be based on a secular foundation and not on a sacred one as was his grandfather's, and he is more concerned with material things in life than with scholarship as was his grandfather. He believes, furthermore, that in life he will not have to work as hard as his grandfather because he is much "smarter" than his grandfather.

Particularly significant is the change in attitude on the part of modern American youth toward family life. He is not as close to his parents, he does not respect them as much, and he is not influenced by them to the degree his parents were by their parents; thus he has contributed heavily to the social changes of the American Jewish family by rebelling against members of the older generation and the familial system they support.

Jewish children, also, are more "spoiled" than non-Jewish children; they are cared for better (this probably explains why Jews rear a greater percentage of children despite the fact that they have smaller numbers); they are given more and are urged to go to college more than non-Jews. They eat more, too, and are heavier than their non-Jewish counterparts. Also, they are more outspoken, are far more interested in social problems, and argue with their teachers more often. The Jewish child does his best to outdress his Gentile friend and often, because deep down he is not certain about his status or position in life, he develops an arrogance and a "smart-aleckness" which defeats the very purpose he is trying to achieve.

Except among the extremely Orthodox children, the attitude toward religion shows a downward trend toward indifference and secularism. Whereas Catholic children are first of all Catholics and Baptist children are first of all Baptists, Jewish children want first of all to be Americans. Most of them are interested in religious activities basically for social reasons. On a bulletin board at the Hillel House at Wisconsin University there is a blunt declaration of its *raison d'etre*: "Meet your spouse at Hillel House."

Most Jewish girls go to college to find eligible Jewish boys, to get "cultured and refined," rather than to get an education or find a vocation, whereas Jewish boys go to college to get training, predominantly in the professions. In both cases the great majority go to prestige schools, but wherever they go they strive intensely to do well.[19]

Noteworthy is the fact that Jewish children "drink" less than non-Jewish children; however, in the matter of "petting" they outdo their non-Jewish counterparts. Some psychologists believe that this pattern of behavior provides an outlet similar to that offered by alcohol to many Gentiles.

On the positive side it may be said that among Jewish children there is less delinquency, gambling, immorality, and divorce. There are more college graduates and more professional people; there is more reading, traveling, and stability in business, and better physical health in general.

Thus it becomes evident that, albeit Jewish parents take good care of their children physically, provide them with a high standard of living, educate them well and prepare them to go out into the rough and tumble of the marketplace, far too many of them are sterilizing themselves emotionally, intellectually, and spiritually in the matter of rearing their children in Jewishness with all that this implies. The result is that many Jewish children are emancipating themselves from

[19] A good example of this may be found at the author's university, which is considered a fairly good school but hardly one of social prestige. Very few Jewish students attend this institution; there are 9,000 students, about fifteen of whom are Jews, and many of these do not admit their Jewishness. The few who come and stay are very serious, and most of them are in the area of engineering.

the old-time "trinity": the synagogue, Judaism, and the family. Indeed, far too many Jewish children reject their past and their traditions looking upon these elements with contempt and often with re-
gret, wishing they could somehow alter them or, better still, erase
them, but without being able to substitute any stable and lasting
dreams or visions for them. So many of these young people, when
adults, live in a psychically twilight world made up of part substance
and part shadow.

It may be said that the real problem facing Jewish children has to
do with their attitude toward Judaism as a religion and Jewishness
as a way of life. Jewish children find themselves in a cultural milieu
which has not yet been clearly defined by Jews; thus they are left
with certain ethnic guideposts which cause them to act in terms of
egocentric and hedonistic patterns which often defeat their long-run
interests and the ideals of their goals in life. This alone could cause
them much mental conflict and emotional frustration and hinder them
from coming to terms with themselves, their religious group, and
with the ever-threatening world around them.[20]

In dealing with the topic of the family one is inclined to regard the
family—and its children. It might be well, at this point, to reverse
the pattern and rearrange the wording: "Children have families."
Beyond the seemingly outworn discussions of the relation of the family to the development of the children is the inescapable implication
found in the ancient principle of the *Tabula Smaragadina*: "What is
above is what is below!" It is the same old theme all over again: the
individual's behavior is immediately determined to a very large degree by his experience, and this depends upon his contact with his
environment, the most important components of which are his family, his culture, and his community. It is particularly within the family that the child develops his self-image, self-esteem, self-evaluation,
and where he generates a degree of ego strength, all of which together

[20] This is profoundly significant in the light of the fact that the health and
stability of an individual requires an integrated personality, which, in turn,
demands stable objects of belief and allegiance. How dramatically true is
this in relation to modern American Jews.

make up his personality resources with which he will have to withstand the gales in the world about him.

Indeed, Jewish children have families and many of these families are sound and stable groups whose Hebraic fabric is still whole and which are able to withstand the forces of modern life and bring to their members purity, peace, faith, courage, integrity, and deep spiritual convictions, those precious ingredients and priceless equipment for solving human problems and for transforming one's relatively sterile materialistic life into one of fruitful existence. These Jews are quite old-fashioned in that they still believe that the soul of man is born fresh in every child, that the God to whom their children say their prayers has a face very much like the faces of their mothers and fathers, and that behind the complicated dicta of the scholars, teachers, sages is the assumption that there exists a difference between good and evil, beauty and ugliness, secular and sacred which is more than a simple affirmation of preference. And, finally, these Jews are simple enough to believe sincerely that being Jewish is not so bad, particularly when one considers the alternatives at this point in man's history.

However, present data are most suggestive that there are equally many Jewish childrens' families which are failing in their basic purpose of rearing their offspring better than they were reared.[21] The real trouble with these families was dramatically expressed by Rabbi Max Maccoby's answer given to the question posed at the 1956 Central Conference of American Rabbis: "How Jewish is the Jewish home?" His answer was: "Not very!" Rabbi Jerome D. Folkman added the disturbing observation that "it would be difficult to distinguish a Jewish home from the typical American except that it would probably be more 'American' than most other homes. . . ." Indeed, both in breadth and in depth the disturbance of the average Jewish family is evident, and the Jewish parent today is not certain whether the ideal of the old Jewish family is something true and worth

[21] Admittedly there is some value judgment involved in this proposition, but it must be noted that there is also a great deal of empirical knowledge involved which cannot be wished away.

preserving or merely a legend which is becoming more of a caricature by the day.

Even a superficial analysis of the situation makes it clear that the basic reason for this condition is the present-day orientation of a large segment of American Jewry. It is important to grasp, at this point, the fundamental fact that man can be understood or can attain understanding only in terms of his inner feelings and not from attributes assigned to him or to his external world. This concept has special significance for those who seek a true comprehension of Judaism and its meaning to its followers in modern America.

In truth, it would be very difficult to delineate those defects in the modern Jewish family which hinder both the development of the Jewish consciousness within its children and the fulfillment of their Jewish goals at both a personal and a group level. It is not only difficult but painful to try to capture the poignant drama that boils underneath the surface of the stress-laden but overtly successful Jewish home and to study the hidden emotional forces that lie behind the behavior patterns of its members.

One of the seriously disturbing elements in the lives of many American Jewish parents today is their breaking away from what may be termed the "Jewish atmosphere"—Jewishness—and their rejection of the basic Judaic ceremonies, without which Judaism loses its power. It must be assumed that the attitude of a person in regard to the rituals of his group is a valid index to his integration into his cultural background.

Ritual indicates special conditions in a family's style of living. The existence of well-organized, well-crystalized, well-established, and well-accepted rituals demonstrates a great amount of likemindedness and cooperation within the group. Such a set of well-structured rituals makes for a continuing and permanent institution, it encourages unity and social control, it facilitates cultural transmission, and, finally, it offers a great deal of psychic satisfaction and generates a special type of fusion of individuals in the common whole. Thus it is that in the midst of the dramatic but disturbing transition from one identity to another in the cultural reality which surrounds them, many American Jewish homes show distinct signs of crumbling away and of dissipating the ideal which has so long been for Jews the only real and lasting force.

Is there an answer to the problem facing the American Jewish family in particular and American Jewry in general? It would take someone with Max Weber's sociological genius, Rabbi Heschel's philosophical insight, and Winston Churchill's eloquence to analyze the problem, to discover the answers, and to put it all down in words. The best this writer can do has been to present a hazy "image" of the problem and give a mere pencil sketch of an answer. Actually, neither the problem nor the solution can be precisely and sharply defined.

This remains certain: if the Jews in America wish to survive as a going concern, it will be necessary for them to participate, long and hard, in a serious search for self-awareness. What is it they really want from Judaism, from their synagogue, and from their families? What is the purpose and *raison d'etre* of being Jewish today? Is there any reality to that mysterious yearning to continue being a part of a system of ideas and values which, for so many, seems to have lost its originality and which has become at best merely a blend of little faith and much skepticism? Is it real, or is it a figment of the imagination, perpetuated by a self-centered group for thousands of years to give them a self-image, a self-dimension, and a self-fulfill-ment which has now run its course? Why not be honest and leave this Jewish microcosm which so many consider an anachronism and sub-stitute the ideals embodied in the Sermon on the Mount for the ideals of Mount Sinai? Surely Christians do not need to be ashamed of their moral and spiritual teachings, perhaps only of their failure to fulfill them. In time Judaism would disappear, as Paul Kresh inti-mated, and people could see its strange remains in some archeological museum.[22]

[22] Arthur Koestler believes that one of the real reasons Jews have hesi-tated to renounce both their religion and their nationalism and to be socially and culturally absorbed by their environment springs essentially from the human tendency to avoid a painful choice. There are other reasons, too, he notes: ". . . spiritual pride, civic courage, the apprehension of being ac-

Or is there something truly sublime and worthwhile in this formula, this *modus vivendi*, which has stood so long in a wasteland of human tissue and human emotions and which can even today preserve and enlarge the dignity of men under conditions in which they must exist?

Jews must this day, then, decide what is their prize in life—and integrity comes high—must realize, painful as it might be, that there are no panaceas for their troubles, no tonics, no opiates, only a return to the dreams, visions, and ethics of Avrom, Moses, Isaiah, Micah, and Amos. And such dreams, visions, and ethics cannot stand up in midair; there must be solid foundations under them, and it will take education and training, courage and commitment, involvement and dedication, self-sacrifice and inspiration to build these foundations, and, finally, an objective search for a deeper comprehension of Judaism and its meaning in man's existence.

While it is true, sociologically speaking, that Judaism is indeed a religion and not a race or nationality, by its very nature, history and development through the ages, it cannot perpetuate itself without the aid of a distinctive culture—a unique pattern of living termed so glibly as "Jewishness." As a mere abstract religious philosophy Judaism would soon become so hemmed in by the pressures from without, so diluted by neighboring influences and so weakened by intermarriage that it could easily, step by step, melt away into something meaningless and worthless. The cultural base must include the history of the Jews, the knowledge of the Bible— not merely the Torah— the Song of Songs, the poetry, the Wisdom of the Fathers, the teachings of the sages, and a participation in the religious holidays and their rituals, plus the basic principles of the Judaic outlook on everyday living.

And how does the family fit into this scheme of things? It is safe to say that children cannot make choices without the guidance of their religious leaders, their teachers, and particularly without that of their

---

cused of hypocrisy or cowardice, the scars of the wounds inflicted in the past, and the reluctance to abandon a mystic destiny, a specifically Jewish mission." Koestler, *The Trail of the Dinosaur*, 115.

parents. In the case of the Jewish family, a religiously motivated home can bring a sense of belonging to its members, its group, and its faith. It can project the family patterns, the age-old hopes and dreams and ideals upon each individual, bringing him confidence in himself and in the universe; it can be the major buffer in easing the tensions which beset him; it can absorb the shocks and tempers each feels in this frightfully competitive society; and it can help resolve the long ambivalence Jews have felt in America, the alternate acceptance of and struggle with irresolution.

Finally, the Jewish family in America can strengthen the ethnic foundations of the Jewish community so that in the uncertain days to come this family group will increase in cohesion as it offers an oasis of understanding, consciousness of kind, moral strength, and spiritual inspiration, and thus raises up the foundations of generations to come. Indeed, it could be that in the seed of this family all nations will be blessed "because thou hast hearkened to my voice."

Perhaps it will be the dramatic epic of the American Jewish family which will prove the truth of the old adage: "As it is written, they who are chosen must first be sorely tried."

IX

Postscriptum

*J*ohn Mason Brown once made the observation that "existence is a strange bargain. Life owes us little—we owe it everything. The only true happiness comes from squandering ourselves for a purpose." Herein lies the crux of the challenge to the current disturbing and paradoxical dilemma of the American Jew and his historical possibilities.

If Judaism is an unreasoned sentiment, a long-established illusion moving blindly through four thousand years, if it is merely a birthmark, then Jews throughout history have surely paid a dear price for a piece of ideological junk. If God is merely an extension of self, and there is no divine government in the universe; if justice, mercy, and humility do not help rule it, and the old Levitical precept "Thou shalt love thy neighbor as thy self" is a farce; if the Hebraic heritage is merely a concoction of ethnocentric myths—then the sanest thing for Jews to do is to crawl back into the jungle, or better still, release the atomic *Golem* they created and turn themselves and their miserable world into the dust and ashes from which they sprang. However, if the contrary is true, then it behooves Jews, as indeed all mankind, to keep alive these ideals and to live by them. A supreme awareness can bring the realization to Jews, at least, that as long as they possess this inheritance and comprehend it, they will be not part of the question in this confused world but part of the answer. This sort of outlook may offer few secular gains but will surely provide the spiritual and intellectual elbowroom one needs to grow and develop sanely and securely. For those who are able to accept its philosophical and ethical requirements, its practice and its discipline, and who are willing to live in its spirit, it offers great reward in serenity of soul, personal fulfillment, courage to stand up for convictions and a view of life which is sublime, distinctive, and beautiful. No one claims that squandering oneself for a purpose is an easy task, but it is a profoundly compensating one.

Rabbi Morris Adler sounds out the ideas eloquently when he says that "the most cherished substance and attainments of Judaism are in the sphere of ideas, values, insights, aspirations; its chief architects are prophets, sages, commentators, philosophers, poets; its key emphasis is 'and these words which I command thee this day shall be upon thy heart and thou shalt teach them diligently unto thy children,' and its foundation is the Torah, a book of institution and law."[1]

How can any Jew rebel against this? There is no mystery here, nothing which takes profound philosophical manipulation, no creed for which room has to be made in the mind by expelling reason from it, no ideas which a child of any color or creed or class cannot grasp with ease.

It is possible that nothing of consequence can be done in regard to the present-day trend of Judaism in America until a new ideology provides a polarization of life and brings with it new hope and faith which will enable Jewry to pick up its old strands and weave them into a fresh and enduring pattern of life. This would mean, first, accepting the very unpleasant fact that neither intellectual training alone, nor brawn, nor material achievements can free the American Jew from the turmoil he is experiencing, and, second, learning the painful yet wonderful lesson all over again that there is no way to achieve that inexplicable phenomenon known as glory without risks and sacrifices. It means, furthermore, going on the offensive; it

[1] Morris Adler, "Learning to Live," *National Jewish Monthly* LXXVIII (January, 1964), 7.

means being as bold, as strong, and as inspired as were those shtetl Jews, and as willing to risk everything for sound and traditional ideals; indeed, it means becoming a challenge rather than an enigma in America and the world.

Most people will agree with the proposition that the future is mostly shaped by men, not alone by nature or supernatural forces and, as far as the future of American Jewry is concerned, the present Jews are those men. No one can be certain what will happen in the future, but whatever happens, this is certain: the present-day Jewish children will inherit it, and what it is they inherit will be determined largely by what is happening to them today in the home, the synagogue, the community, and on the campus. If their parents, teachers, and community leaders have the power and the inspiration and the courage to fulfill the promise of the Judaic ideal then these children will have much to bring to the future. If not, they will find themselves on a strange treadmill, wearing themselves out in the effort to conform to the point of totalitarianism and all that it implies, creating masks and self-delusions in order to hide the earthly clay which once reflected the images of God, realizing, as time goes by, that they do not feel, hope, suffer, or even despair with any intensity.

There may be many answers to the dilemma facing American Jewry; however, there is one answer that is certain and that is *action*. Jews in America can ill afford to continue along this long, lonely and, in many ways, unlovely stretch of spiritual wasteland. Whatever the action it must begin very near for the simple reason that one cannot go very far if he does not begin very near. Someone or some group must systematically set forth a new frame of living, new guideposts, new directions and a new body of values (name the movement what you will), and a blueprint for living which could possibly mobilize each Jew's scattered energies into one triumphant sense of his own infinite importance in the scheme of things, be it his family, his synagogue, his community, his state, his nation, his universe.

Oddly enough, there is such a movement in America and it is near. It has a relatively small following at this point, but it does give a new definition to Judaism. It is beginning to exert wide influence, and

it is this writer's opinion that within this frame of Judaism Jews can
re-establish themselves. It is called Reconstructionist Judaism. Rabbi
Mordecai Kaplan was its founder and is still its guiding spirit. As
Rabbi E. S. Goldsmith explains:

> Rabbi Kaplan's philosophy and program illumines Judaism in three
> dimensions: the existential dimension of Jewish people-hood, the essential
> dimension of Jewish religion, and the functional dimension of the Jew-
> ish way of living. It teaches that the meaning of Jewish existence is to be
> a People in the image of God, and that the purpose of Jewish life is for
> us to foster in ourselves as Jews and to waken in the rest of the world, a
> sense of moral responsibility in action. It seeks to help modern man over-
> come some of the disastrous illusions that he has uncritically accepted,
> such as "rugged individualism," "total collectivism," and the "unchange-
> ability of human nature."[2]

After many years of critical reflection on the condition of American Jewish life, this writer is of the opinion that there is more than
a mere hint on the horizon of the descending twilight of Judaism and
the Jewish family. As a child the writer lived within the truly Orthodox tradition, and his adult life has been spent actively within a
"pure" Reform atmosphere. He is convinced that Orthodox Judaism
has little meaning in terms of life's operations in modern America
and that Reform Judaism lacks those certain ingredients which could
enable Jews to escape from the anonymity of their secular life. What
is needed is an awakening of the old Hebraic spirit within the framework of modern Americana. American Jewry can draw its strength
from the deep well of Judaic tradition, it can filter it through the
sieve of modern life, and it can come up with the living water of a
new faith—a faith which can still include the thunder and lightning
of the fierce Moses, the brevity of Amos, the lucidity of Micah, the
poetry and music of David, and the depth of Isaiah. Thoreau expressed the idea beautifully in *Walden* when he said: "We must
learn to awaken and keep ourselves awake, not by mechanical aids

[2] E. S. Goldsmith, "Reconstructionist Judaism," *National Jewish Monthly*,
LXXIX (June, 1965), 4. See also Mordecai M. Kaplan, *Judaism As a Civilization* (New York: Macmillan Co., 1934).

but by an infinite expectation of the dawn. . . ." Jews must now choose between waiting for the twilight or waiting for the dawn. No one can choose for them.

For this writer the die is cast, the way points to the path staked out by Rabbi Kaplan and made passable by his followers. Here is a pattern which can awaken American Jewry and help it emerge from the wilderness of the lost and from the chaotic individualism and secularism of modern life. Here is a religious philosophy based on the breadth and depth of the Hebraic foundation, slightly transcendental in thought, with the spread of idealistic sociology as one of its goals, making of it a pattern which encourages not only a new knowledge but also a fresh insight. It is a formula which emphasizes man's intellectual capacity as well as his moral capacity, which holds out not only for individual responsibility but family and group responsibility; a formula which will prove for American Jews a means by which they might find the power, wisdom, energy and glory to combat the forces crowding them from all sides and from all sources. Indeed it could give reality to the symbolic implication of Rosh Hashanah, the yearning for the divine gift of redemption and to man's attempt to be entitled to it. It could open men's eyes to the miraculous dimension implied in the old Hebrew song *Hatikva* (hope); and finally it could help tune their ears, hearts, and minds to the ancient call of the Shofar: *"Na'ashe Ve' nishma"*—"We will do and we will learn."

Somewhere in the spirit of man, far from the Orthodox synagogue and from the Reform temple, far from the office, the golf course, the home, and the highway, there is a place where God resides. He neither loves nor hates, really, for these things come and go, change and pass away. He neither asks the reader nor answers the writer. He merely surveys the universe He created a trillion years ago to the trillionth power, and exercises His laws which are immutable and which somehow bring both a tragic and a beautiful dimension to each man as he passeth by.

If and when Judaism and Jews disappear from the scene, as do all social groups sooner or later, this can be said of these incredible people as the curtain falls on the drama of the wandering Jew. Theirs at least was not a short dream, a blind dream, a meaningless dream. If their sun sets and their moon no longer rises, and their stars no longer shine in the heavens, and though in the end they will have failed, they had the promise of a long dream, a soul-stirring dream, a stubborn, determined and yet tender dream—a dream not of a day, or a year, or even a century, but of the ages.

Selected References

Abrahams, Gerald. *The Jewish Mind*. Boston: Beacon Press, 1961.

Abrahams, Israel. *Jewish Life in the Middle Ages*. New York: Meridian Books, 1961.

Aleichem, Sholem. *The Old Country*. New York: Crown Publishing Company, 1946.

Anshen, Ruth N. (ed.). *The Family: Its Function and Destiny*. New York: Harper and Brothers, 1959.

Ausubel, Nathan. *The Book of Jewish Knowledge*. New York: Crown Publishers, Inc., 1964.

Baeck, Leo. *The Essence of Judaism*. New York: Schocken Books, 1948.

Bamberger, Bernard J. *The Bible: A Modern Jewish Approach*. New York: Schocken Books, 1963.

Baron, Salo W. *The Jewish Community*. Philadelphia: Jewish Publication Society of America, 1945.

Beauvoir, Simone de. *The Second Sex*. New York: Alfred A. Knopf, 1953.

Bentwitch, Norman. *The Jews in Our Time*. Baltimore: Penguin Books, 1960.

Berkson, Isaac B. *Theories of Americanization*. New York: Teachers' College, Columbia University, 1920.

Bevan, E. R. and Charles Singer (eds.). *The Legacy of Israel*. London: Oxford University Press, 1927.

Bickerman, Elias. *Ezra to the Last of the Maccabees.* New York: Schocken Books, 1962.

Bokser, Ben Zim. *Wisdom of the Talmud.* New York: The Citadel Press, 1962.

Bridger, David (ed.). *The New Jewish Encyclopedia.* New York: Behrman House, Inc., 1962.

Bruno, Ezra S. "The Emigrant Jews at Home," in *The World's Work.* New York: Doubleday, Page and Company, 1903.

Buber, Martin. *Israel and the World.* New York: Schocken Books, 1963.

Burgess, Ernest W. and Harvey Locke. *The Family.* New York: American Book Company, 1953.

Cohen, Raphael. *Reflections of a Wondering Jew.* Boston: Beacon Press, 1950.

Davidson, Marshall B. (ed.). *The Horizon Book of Lost Worlds.* New York: American Heritage Publishing Company, 1962.

Demiashkevich, Michael. *The National Mind.* New York: American Book Company, 1938.

Durant, Will. *Our Oriental Heritage.* New York: Simon and Schuster, 1954.

Eisendrath, Maurice N. *Can Faith Survive?* New York: McGraw-Hill Book Company, 1964.

Epstein, Isidore, *Judaism: A Historical Presentation.* Baltimore: Penguin Books, 1959.

Erskine, John. *Adam and Eve.* Indianapolis: Bobbs-Merrill Company, 1927.

Ewer, W. M. *Modern Humor.* New York: Citadel Press, 1945.

Feldman, W. M. *The Jewish Child.* London: Bailliere, Tindall, and Cox, 1917.

Fine, Morris and Milton Himmelfarb (eds.). *American Jewish Yearbook, 1963.* Philadelphia: Jewish Publication Society of America, 1963.

Finkelstein, Louis (ed.). *The Jews.* New York: Harper and Row, 1950.

Friedman, Bruce Jay. *A Mother's Kisses.* New York: Simon and Schuster, 1964.

Ginzberg, Louis. *The Legend of the Jews.* Philadelphia: Jewish Publication Society of America, 1912.

Glatzer, Nahum N. (ed.). *Hammer on the Rocks: A Midrash Reader.* New York: Shocken Books, 1962.

Glazer, Nathan, and Daniel Patrick Moynihan. *Beyond the Melting Pot.* Cambridge, Mass.: M.I.T. Press and Harvard University Press, 1964.

Goldin, Judah (ed.). *The Wisdom of the Fathers.* New York: Heritage Press, 1957.

Goldstein, S. E. *Meaning of Marriage and Foundations of the Family: A Jewish Interpretation.* New York: Bloch Publishing Company, 1942.

Gordon, Milton M. *Assimilation in American Life.* New York: Oxford University Press, 1964.

Graves, Robert and Raphael Patai. *Hebrew Myths: The Book of Genesis.* Garden City: Doubleday and Company, 1964.

Hebert, Gabriel. *The Old Testament from Within.* London: Oxford University Press, 1962.

Herberg, Will. *Judaism and Modern Man.* New York: Meridian Books, Inc., 1959.

————. *Protestant–Catholic–Jew.* Garden City: Anchor Books, 1960.

Hersey, John. *The Wall.* New York: Alfred A. Knopf, 1950.

Hertz, Joseph Herman (ed.). *The Voice of Prayer: A Book of Thoughts.* New York: Bloch Publishing Company, 1943.

Heschel, Abraham Joshua. *The Earth Is the Lord's.* New York: Henry Schuman, 1950.

Hoffer, Eric. *The True Believer.* New York: Mentor Books, 1962.

Horton, Paul B., and Chester L. Hunt. *Sociology.* New York: McGraw-Hill Book Company, 1964.

Idelsohn, Abraham Z. *The Ceremonies of Judaism.* Cincinnati: National Federation of Temple Brotherhoods, 1930.

James, William. *Psychology.* New York: Henry Holt and Company,

Jennep, Arnold van. *The Rites of Passage.* Chicago: University of Chicago Press, 1960.

Kaplan, Benjamin. *The Eternal Stranger.* New York: Bookman, 1957.

Kaplan, Mordecai M. *The Future of the American Jew.* New York: Macmillan Company, 1948.

————. *Judaism As a Civilization.* New York: Macmillan Company, 1934.

Keller, Werner. *The Bible As History.* New York: William Morrow and Company, 1958.

Klausner, Joseph. *Jesus of Nazareth.* New York: Macmillan Company, 1957.

Koestler, Arthur. *The Trail of the Dinosaur and Other Essays.* New York: Macmillan Company, 1955.

Kramer, Judith R., and Seymour Leventman. *Children of the Gilded Ghetto.* New Haven: Yale University Press, 1961.

Langdon, Stephen Herberg. "Semitic," in Vol. V of *The Mythology of All Races.* Boston: Marshall Jones Company, 1931.

McCarthy, Justin, et al. *World's Great Classics: Hebrew Literature.* New York: Colonial Press, 1901.

McKenzie, John L. *The Two-Edged Sword.* Milwaukee: Bruce Publishing Company, 1955.

Margolis, Max L. and Alexander Marx. *A History of the Jewish People.* Philadelphia: Jewish Publication Society of America, 1927.

Marx, Karl. *A World Without Jews.* New York: Philosophical Library, 1959.

Moehlman, Conrad Henry. *The Christian-Jewish Tragedy: A Study in Religious Prejudice.* New York: Leo Hart, 1933.

Montagu, Ashley. *The Natural Superiority of Women.* New York: Macmillan Company, 1953.

Mowrer, O. Hobart. *The Crises in Psychiatry and Religion.* New York: Van Nostrand, 1961.

Nimkoff, M. F. (ed.). *Comparative Family Systems.* Boston: Houghton Mifflin Company, 1965.

Noveck, Simon (ed.). *Contemporary Jewish Thought.* Washington: B'nai B'rith Department of Adult Jewish Education, 1963.

———— (ed.). *Great Jewish Personalities in Modern Times.* Washington: B'nai B'rith Department of Adult Jewish Education, 1964.

Peretz, Isaac Leib. *Stories and Pictures.* Philadelphia: Jewish Publication Society of America, 1906.

Peters, Madison C. *Justice to the Jews.* New York: McClure Company, 1908.

Pfeiffer, Robert H. *Introduction to the Old Testament.* New York: Harper and Row, 1943.

Phillips, Derek. L. (ed.). *Studies in American Society.* New York: Thomas Y. Crowell Company, 1960.

Pittman, David J. and Charles R. Snyder (eds.). *Society, Culture, and Drinking Patterns.* New York: John Wiley and Sons, Inc., 1962.

Redkin, Michael L. (ed.). *Babylonian Talmud.* Boston: The Talmudic Society, 1918.

Ribalow, Harold U. *The Jew in American Sports.* New York: Bloch Publishing Company, 1959.

Rischin, Moses. *The Promised City*. New York: Corinth Books, 1964.

Rosenberg, Stuart E. *America Is Different*. New York: Thomas Nelson and Sons, 1964.

Roth, Henry. *Call It Sleep*. New York: Avon Books, 1964.

Salinger, J. D. *Franny and Zooey*. Boston: Little, Brown and Company, 1961.

Sandmel, Samuel. *The Hebrew Scriptures*. New York: Alfred A. Knopf, 1963.

Schiirer, Emil. *A History of the Jewish People in the Time of Jesus Christ*. New York: Charles Scribner's Sons, 1891.

Sherman, C. Bezalel. *The Jew Within American Society*. Detroit: Wayne University Press, 1961.

Simpson, George E. and J. Milton Yinger. *Racial and Cultural Minorities*. New York: Harper and Brothers, 1953.

Singer, Isaac Bashevis. *The Slave*. New York: Farrar, Straus, and Cudahy, 1962.

Steinberg, Milton. *A Partisan Guide to the Jewish Problem*. New York: Bobbs-Merrill Company, 1945.

Stephens, William N. *The Family in Cross-Cultural Perspective*. New York: Holt, Rinehart, and Winston, Inc., 1963.

Sullivan, Harry Stack. *Conception of Modern Psychiatry*. Washington: William A. White Foundation, 1947.

Tarshish, Allan. *Not by Power*. New York: Bookman Associates, 1952.

Tietze, F. J. and J. E. McKeowen. *The Changing Metropolis*. Boston: Houghton Mifflin Company, 1964.

Vaihinger, H. *The Philosophy of 'As If.'* New York: Harcourt, Brace, and Company, 1925.

Waller, Walter and Reuben Hill. *The Family*. New York: Dryden Press, 1956

Weber, Max. *Ancient Judaism*. Glencoe, Illinois: The Free Press, 1952.

Week, James. *Hebrew Origins*. New York: Harper and Brothers, 1950.

Williams, Robin M. *Strangers Next Door*. Englewood Cliffs: Prentice Hall, Inc., 1964.

Wirth, Louis. *The Ghetto*. Chicago: University of Chicago Press, 1928.

Zangwill, Israel. *Dreamers of the Ghetto*. New York: Bloch Publishing Company, 1923.

Zborowski, Mark and Elizabeth Herzog. *Life Is with People*. New York: International Universities Press, 1952.

Index